CANADA AND THE UKRAINIAN CRISIS

Canada and
the Ukrainian Crisis

BOHDAN S. KORDAN
and MITCHELL C.G. DOWIE

McGill-Queen's University Press
Montreal & Kingston • London • Chicago

© McGill-Queen's University Press 2020

ISBN 978-0-2280-0134-8 (cloth)
ISBN 978-0-2280-0135-5 (paper)
ISBN 978-0-2280-0273-4 (ePDF)
ISBN 978-0-2280-0274-1 (ePUB)

Legal deposit fourth quarter 2020
Bibliothèque nationale du Québec

Printed in Canada on acid-free paper that is 100% ancient forest free (100% post-consumer recycled), processed chlorine free

This book has been published with the help of a grant from the Publications Fund at St Thomas More College and from the BCU Foundation.

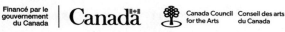

We acknowledge the support of the Canada Council for the Arts.

Nous remercions le Conseil des arts du Canada de son soutien.

Library and Archives Canada Cataloguing in Publication

Title: Canada and the Ukrainian crisis / Bohdan S. Kordan and Mitchell C.G. Dowie.

Names: Kordan, Bohdan S., author. | Dowie, Mitchell C. G., 1989– author.

Description: Includes bibliographical references and index.

Identifiers: Canadiana (print) 20200299476 | Canadiana (ebook) 20200299670 | ISBN 9780228001355 (softcover) | ISBN 9780228001348 (hardcover) | ISBN 9780228002734 (PDF) | ISBN 9780228002741 (ePUB)

Subjects: LCSH: Canada—Foreign relations—Ukraine. | LCSH: Ukraine—Foreign relations—Canada. | LCSH: Ukraine—History—Euromaidan Protests, 2013–2014. | LCSH: Ukraine—History—21st century. | CSH: Canada—Politics and government—2006–2015. | CSH: Canada—Politics and government—2015–

Classification: LCC FC251.U38 K67 2020 | DDC 327.710477—dc23

This book was typeset by Marquis Interscript in 10/13 Sabon.

To Danya and Christian,
Shirley and Patrick
With love and respect

Contents

Preface   ix

Acknowledgments   xiii

Introduction   3

1   International Order and Canadian Aspirations:
An Appreciation   12

2   The Ukrainian Crisis, Canada, and World Order: Systemic
Imperatives and the Canadian Response   28

3   The Crisis and Canadian Interests: Canada's Support
for Ukraine   45

4   The Leadership of Stephen Harper: Agency, Worldview,
and the Ukrainian Crisis   65

5   Stephen Harper's Ukraine Policy: Toward
an Understanding   84

The Harper Government's Response to the Ukrainian Crisis:
A Chronology   97

Notes   111

Index   137

Preface

In the latter half of the twentieth century, two major theoretical frameworks dominated the academic field of international relations. Liberal internationalism would recognize the important part that democracy, free trade, and multilateralism played in achieving a postwar peace dividend. In contrast, political realism emphasized the strategic importance of power and national interest in a competitive global system. During the Cold War, the majority of Canadian scholars used one or the other doctrine to help situate and explain Canada's foreign policy. By 2014–15, however, these proved limited in addressing the changing nature of international relations and the reworked assumptions behind Canada's strategic and political interests. This constituted a serious shortcoming. Indeed, regarding Canada's response under Prime Minister Stephen Harper to Russia's aggression against Ukraine in 2014, these frameworks either failed to accurately capture the meaning, dynamics, and substance of what was at issue, or gave rise to speculative narratives about the Harper government's response.

Two accounts, in particular, stand out. The first casts the crisis as part of a wider debate about the West's bellicose behaviour, which, it is said, unfairly targets Russia. The critics argue that Russia's behaviour is in fact part of the normal functioning of the international system. Canadian interests, therefore, are best served by accepting the former's stature as a great power. Canada, they contend, should not permit itself to be drawn needlessly into a matter of little national importance or consequence. The second attributes the government's policy response to the allegedly outsized influence of the Ukrainian-Canadian diaspora and the need to gain electoral favour with this constituency. This community, with its political agenda, is said to be the driving force behind Canada's robust partisan support for Ukraine, adversely affecting its traditional approach as an international arbiter.

Both assessments, however, are deeply flawed. One downplays Canada's enduring interest in and commitment to a liberal order grounded in rights, obliging us to consider the response as part of a wider historical and political concern. The other fails to recognize that the basis for the community/government relationship is a shared understanding of the problem, which has led to overlapping interests and cooperation. If we are to fully understand Canada's response to the Ukrainian crisis, an analysis that considers and fully describes the nature of these developments is needed. The importance of adopting a more complete and nuanced interpretation cannot be overstated. The crisis in Ukraine continues and Canadian troops – advisors and trainers alike – remain stationed there. How did we get to this point? What is at stake? Does the same rationale that gave rise to the Harper government's response still apply?

We acknowledge that the world is increasingly defined by rapid and significant change, and that Russia's attempt at rewriting the international rules of the road represents a particular challenge to Canada's interests. As such, we seek to advance a perspective that does not gloss over the importance or centrality of this challenge. It is also a perspective that remains sensitive to the way that change has informed the manner in which Canadian leadership, with its own preferences, interpreted the Ukrainian crisis while taking into consideration Canada's traditional strategic and political interests. In addition, the perspective seeks to understand more completely, in light of the crisis, the basis of the relationship between government and community. All of this has methodological and analytical significance. Indeed, they way in which variables at the international, national, and individual levels combine to produce Canada's foreign policy response to the Ukrainian crisis will frame our discussion. We believe this layered approach will offer insights that can best explain Canada's actions in this instance.

The claim made here is that Canada's foreign policy sought to adapt to uncertainty and was modified in the process. Yet, the policy that resulted was less a departure from and more a return to traditional postwar concerns about the international system and the threats facing it. To be sure, Canada's reaction reflected the preferences of Prime Minister Harper and signalled the country's support for principles embedded in the existing order that mirrored its longstanding foreign policy interests and goals. But it was also the case that the nature of the threat and its implications for global stability and security reinforced the prime minister's worldview and reaffirmed those interests. The following analysis seeks to understand this dynamic, which led to a policy response that was striking yet emblematic of the dynamic interaction that would occur between global change, state interests, and the personalities involved.

Acknowledgments

This book began with a question: What accounts for the robustness of Canada's response during the Ukrainian crisis? It is a modest question but one laden with profound implications. In answering it, we were led to reflect on other issues and concerns. How is it that Ukraine represents an important security interest for Canada? Does the Ukrainian-Canadian community wield influence in Canadian foreign policy? And more broadly still, in the Canadian context, what is the nature of the relationship between diasporas and government? These sorts of questions framed our ruminations and deliberations. We discovered that the answers were neither simple nor immediately evident. Rather, our investigations highlighted the complexity of these issues. This book is a short statement on the nature of Canada's response to the crisis in Ukraine and the environment in which the decisions relating to it were made. Not everyone will agree with our analysis or assessment. But it is a starting point – one which takes us beyond cliché and speculation.

Throughout the course of our investigations, we received much encouragement, support, and assistance. We gratefully acknowledge the contributions of Kris Pikl, who read the manuscript and made suggestions and recommendations. We are indebted to our colleagues at the Prairie Centre for the Study of Ukrainian Heritage at St Thomas More College, University of Saskatchewan, and the Ramon Hnatyshyn Canadian Studies Centre at Chernivtsi National

University, Ukraine. Both centres offered us a fertile home environment conducive to research and writing. Publication of this book was made possible through the Publications Fund at St Thomas More College and a generous grant from the BCU Foundation.

The publication process is long and complicated. From start to finish, years pass before a book finally emerges into the light of day. This cannot occur, however, without the commitment and support of the publisher and those who work on its behalf. We are grateful to McGill-Queen's University Press and its staff for the kindness and consideration shown to us. In particular, we are indebted to Jacqueline Mason, editor, for her unstinting perseverance and allegiance to the project. Kathleen Fraser, Joanne Pisano, and Paloma Friedman all helped in managing various aspects of the publication process. The wordsmith on this manuscript was the talented Edwin Janzen, who expertly wielded his copyeditor's pen. His skill is recognized here with great appreciation and humility.

Writing is usually a solitary affair. Thankfully, we had one another as co-authors. But we also had the support and encouragement of family. No words can express the profound gratitude and esteem in which we hold our families. It is they who pardoned our indulgences and commiserated with us as we carried on with our labours. Although it is a small gesture, with this dedication we reaffirm our great love and deep respect for all they have done and all they continue to do.

CANADA AND THE UKRAINIAN CRISIS

Introduction

Since 1991, Canada has enjoyed a special relationship with Ukraine that has seen successive Canadian governments – Liberal and Conservative – provide this newly independent state with ongoing economic aid and political assistance. While relations have remained resilient and consistent throughout, there were occasions where Canada demonstrated exceptional support.[1] The year 2014 was one such moment, when, responding to Russia's aggression against Ukraine, Prime Minister Stephen Harper took measures expressing Canada's solidarity with the new Ukrainian government while demonstrating Canada's disapproval of and opposition to Russia's actions. The prime minister's robust declarations and actions were conspicuous, particularly in view of the apparent reduced attention given by the Liberal government to the crisis after the Conservatives' electoral defeat in 2015. Indeed, although there would be operational continuity in the policy pursued by the Liberal government of Justin Trudeau, Canada's response in its dispute with Russia has been relatively quiet and restrained. This has remained the case even after Chrystia Freeland – a stalwart of the Ukrainian-Canadian community – assumed the role of Canada's foreign minister.[2] This suggests to us that the Harper government's response may have been an anomaly.

At a certain level, the strong Canadian support for Ukraine during its moment of need can be explained as the result of Canada's much-touted propensity to "do good" in the world. Canada's image as a benevolent international actor that strives to make a positive difference reflects a genuine sentimentality about its identity, one that is deeply rooted in the principles and values embedded in Canadian political culture: democracy, freedom, justice, and, more recently, pluralism, equality, and tolerance. While this may provide some indication of the motivations undergirding Canadian foreign policy, it still does not account for the nuanced policy differences that exist between governments. Thus, the idea of Canada as a noble, selfless, and altruistic actor is of limited value in understanding change in Canadian foreign policy. Beliefs and national identity may only account for part of the story.

Indeed, while Canada has been referred to as a progressive and even "post-national" state, it remains the case that it is still a state. As such, it has the same political, security, and economic interests as any other state in the modern era. Moreover, it has consistently advanced these traditional interests, regardless of which party governs or how its foreign policy is framed. There are, of course, competing interpretations of what exactly constitutes the national interest, reflecting the extended debates following the end of the Cold War.[3] Nevertheless, preserving Canadian security is hardly an altruistic policy motivation. It is one born of pragmatism and calculated self-interest. Even proponents of the view that Canada is a selfless actor are forced to concede that the country cannot position itself to "do good" in the world if it does not first attend to the more basic task of maintaining and advancing its security.

Since security is a central concern of modern statecraft, the Harper government's policy during the Ukrainian crisis could be viewed as a given. However, the prime minister's decision to unambiguously assert Canada's security interests in this case was unusual insofar as it was considered to be a departure from the views and approaches of previous governments. This apparent break with the past raises a few questions. What was the nature of the crisis that elicited such a response? How did Ukraine come to be such an important Canadian security interest during this period? What role did the leadership of Stephen Harper play? And, more fundamentally, was the nature of the Harper government's response so different from past governments?

Introduction

A few observations are in order if the centrality of these questions is to be appreciated. First, any analysis of the Harper government's Ukraine policy during the crisis should consider the wider context in which it was framed. The international political system is a highly structured affair and is governed by norms and expectations that are intended to create certainty and minimize risk. These conditions highlight the deep connection between the structure of the international system and state behaviour, as well as the role of crises in altering the trajectory of international politics. Second, the Harper government's response to the Ukrainian crisis was not the only available option. The change in tack under the Trudeau government was evidence that there were other approaches to managing the situation. This difference stems from diverging perceptions about the opportunities and constraints that at once guide the pursuit of Canada's interests and limit its strategic options. Third, the concept of leadership implies that individual agency is at work. Agency points to worldview and underlines the fact that a leader's ideas, experiences, and values can and often do play a role in defining a government's expectations and policy preferences in response to perceived threats.

Based on these observations, an additional series of more specific questions arises. For example, which incentives and constraints shaped Canada's foreign policy interests and approach to dealing with the security challenge posed by Russia's aggression? How were these interpreted and what measures were taken? Furthermore, as leader, what role did Stephen Harper's beliefs, values, and experiences play in Canada's response to the Ukrainian crisis? Finally, how do these variables combine to help explain Canada's approach to the crisis under Prime Minister Harper, and which of them, if any, are the most significant? Let us consider the following.

The start of 2014 ushered in a period of unexpected political change in Ukraine when the Ukrainian parliament, the *Rada*, restored constitutional order after the country's discredited president, Victor Yanukovych, was routed by the Euromaidan, a civic movement that demanded transparency, accountability, and responsibility. Russia, which staunchly opposed these developments, looked to take advantage of the instability in Ukraine by occupying and annexing Crimea. Russia then sponsored an insurgency, deploying mercenaries as well as regulars to fight alongside separatists in the country's eastern territories (all the while denying their existence and participation), thus further destabilizing the situation. These acts of aggression were roundly denounced as a serious threat to global peace and security.

While Canada joined other states in censuring Russia's actions, there was a boldness to the Harper government's denunciations and accusations that set it apart, not only from the rest of the international community but also from the foreign policy practice of previous Canadian governments. Some observers characterized the government's position – made clear on several occasions by the prime minister – as belligerent and uncompromising. In this regard, Prime Minister Harper's worldview and politics appear to have been profoundly shaped by what has been described as "moral imperative," or the determination to do right. Moreover, it has been suggested that the prime minister's "moral clarity" – a form of situational awareness – allowed him to intuit and respond to this threat in an unapologetic and forthright manner.[4] In contrast to statements that would have been more conducive to a politically expedient course of action, Stephen Harper's candid and bellicose pronouncements – echoing the earlier Cold War rhetoric of Ronald Reagan and Margaret Thatcher – signalled his desire to position Canada unequivocally on the "right side of history."[5]

Arguably, the prime minister's intentions with regard to the Ukrainian crisis, made clear through his public statements and actions, foregrounded the central role of leadership in shaping Canada's response.[6] Leadership in this instance played a decisive role and is useful for gaining insight into the ideas and value systems that often motivate leaders. But it also invites some significant questions and comparisons. For example: upon what was the strength of Prime Minister Harper's convictions based and were they as pivotal as we are led to believe? Moreover, what impact did global developments and state interests have on the prime minister's predilections and preferences?

We are reminded that, although the views and policies of politicians are informed by belief systems, their decisions are ultimately influenced by a broader set of considerations. Indeed, national leaders must keep the interests of their own country and the motivations of other states in mind while simultaneously contending not only with the incentives and constraints of a competitive world system but domestic interests and pressures as well. A nation's political culture, for example, can play a significant role in foreign policy making, guiding leadership decisions. Additionally, although foreign policy makers may be mindful of the dynamics of state interaction and the costs associated with a foreign policy that fails to take into account state interests, their behaviour and expectations are influenced strongly by the nature of the global system, which is not static. This implies some level of sensitivity to change – or the possibility of change – in the system. All of this points to the interaction that takes place between the existing order, state interests, and political leadership. So how, then, are we to make sense of a process in which these factors operate simultaneously and in tandem?

Neoclassical realism provides a useful theoretical framework to understand this process.[7] Although assigning analytical primacy to the structure of the international order, the theory acknowledges that factors at the national and individual levels can and often do play an intervening role. This helps to explain why some states, in pursuing their foreign policy interests, might choose to participate in a coalition that seeks to preserve the system as constructed, while others may look to reconfigure it. The model is further able to illuminate how the failure to respond to such strategic imperatives by leaders can ultimately jeopardize a state's survival and how the perceived gaps between commitments and capabilities inform the strategic imagination of foreign policy makers.[8] Most importantly, neoclassical realism drills down into the idea that these factors do not function in isolation – that shifts in the distribution of power at the international level necessitate foreign policy decisions without dictating their content. This is so because the calculus underlying foreign policy decisions incorporates leadership perspectives and takes into account state interests. As such, domestic factors and the perceptions of decision makers can be factors in how states respond to events on the world stage and may explain the variation that occurs.

Although neoclassical realism invites us to consider how second-tier variables impact the decision-making process, it also makes clear that political change and developments at the global level are pivotal. Neoclassical realism emphasizes that abrupt change, or the threat of change, to the existing power balance is central to the foreign policy–making process and that state interests and leadership perspectives revolve around this issue. Thus, even though Canada's relationship with Ukraine prior to the crisis was not a priority interest for the Harper government, once the crisis erupted the Canada-Ukraine relationship was quickly elevated to the top of Canada's foreign policy agenda.[9] Representing a rapid and significant shift in the government's international priorities, it is unlikely that such movement would have occurred were it not for the implications of the crisis vis-à-vis the international order.

Importantly, while the key questions regarding Prime Minister Harper's response relate to change, it is worth noting that his approach did not necessarily represent an absolute departure from Canada's foreign policy past or tradition. The international circumstances that Harper had to contend with were dramatically different from those that existed during the tenure of other prime ministers. Left unchecked, Russia's actions would pose an existential threat to the rules-based order. Demanding an energetic response, it was natural that the prime minister's rhetoric would differ from that of his predecessors, who formulated their foreign policies during a period of relative geopolitical stability. This suggests to us that the Harper government's approach might be more properly understood as being in keeping with the traditional Canadian preoccupation with international security and stability, and that the difference, therefore, was more a matter of degree rather than kind.

No less important was the government's relationship with the Ukrainian-Canadian community during the crisis. To the extent that the government would share with the community certain objectives – notably the preservation of Ukrainian sovereignty

Introduction

and independence – there existed a synergy between the two. This points to the government's longstanding practice of consulting and cooperating with this community, highlighting continuity in policy. Still, there is no disputing the fact that the Harper government differed from past governments. Its rhetoric alone was sharper, and therefore indicative of something new and unusual. This underscores the distinctive nature of the prime minister's understanding of the broader external threat, and the role that opportunities, circumstances, and principles would play in shaping Canada's response.

The opening chapter of this book presents a general discussion of Canada's post–Cold War interests as a state committed to promoting the ideas and principles that underpinned the liberal order and how systemic change, specifically the collapse of the USSR, led the Western coalition to shift its foreign policy orientation from defending this system to consolidating it. The chapter details how, within the context of the Soviet collapse and its attendant uncertainties, the interests of Canada and newly independent Ukraine would crystallize around the issue of support for a rules-based order led by the US. In the process, Canada's bilateral relationship with Ukraine would strengthen, underlining the impact of the global context on Canadian foreign policy.

Chapter 2 outlines the ways in which systemic change continued to influence the foreign policy process – particularly the unexpected security challenge that Russia's aggression against Ukraine posed to the post–Cold War liberal order. Highlighting the critical role of global change on the foreign policy–making process, the chapter examines the Harper government's assessment of Russia's violation of Ukraine's sovereignty in view of the requirements of preserving the existing international order and Canada's strategic role within a US-led coalition supporting that order. The coalition's return to a Cold War–style defensive posture would reflect a strategic environment reminiscent of the earlier Cold War rivalry and thus underscore the continuity in Canada's foreign policy.

In chapter 3, consideration is given not only to the incentives and constraints that conditioned the government's perception of the country's national interests, but also how these helped form its assessment of the threat while shaping the measures to be taken during the Ukrainian crisis. Focusing on the Harper government's commitment to and support for principles embedded in the liberal order and the country's political culture, the chapter examines how these principles were framed as national interests, which, being tied to values, led to specific assistance initiatives throughout the crisis.

Chapter 4 evaluates the role of agency and discusses how Stephen Harper's worldview – outlined by an unconditional understanding of America's global role and his beliefs and values system – conditioned his government's response to the Ukrainian crisis and imparted an element of robustness to its position and behaviour. Of interest here are domestic political developments – specifically the rise of conservative populism in Canada – which not only shaped the prime minister's strategic understanding of Canada's national interests but also his ideological take on world developments and the moral obligation to respond to threats.

The final chapter concludes with an assessment of the nature and character of Stephen Harper's Ukraine policy while highlighting the dynamic process that existed between the shifting global power structure, national interests, and political leadership. Throughout the book, the nature of the Harper government's connection to the Ukrainian-Canadian community is also assessed and explained.

This study aims to advance an understanding of the rapid, disruptive changes that shaped the direction of Canada's foreign policy engagement with Ukraine. Russia's invasion of Ukraine in 2014 constituted a threat to the rules-based order. This elicited a vigorous response from the Harper government and placed Canada at the centre of the effort to defend the post–Cold War system. The forcefulness of Canada's reaction was unexpected. Moreover, its subsequent role in the Ukrainian crisis did not conform to the widely accepted but largely idealized image of Canada as a "helpful fixer" or "honest broker." Yet, its approach was entirely consistent with the principles and values associated with the international order created in 1945 and with Canada's foreign policy past, which committed it to stand firm with a coalition of states in support of the status quo and with the US as the system leader. It would also enable the government to work closely and in line with a diaspora that was just as committed to seeing Russia's aggression reversed. Given the significance of the threat, the Canadian approach to the Ukrainian crisis represented a coherent response – one that mirrored Stephen Harper's ideological and moral stance in regard to the necessity of defending principles seen as being at the heart of both Canada's identity and interest in a rules-based order. It is this combination, ultimately, that would lend a sense of urgency and fervour to Canada's response.

1

International Order and Canadian Aspirations: An Appreciation

Canada has consistently supported the international order created in 1945. This inclination stems from the benefits derived from the sense of certainty that is the result of international stability. However, Canada and its allies were also inclined to support and defend this order and its foundational rules because they embodied ideas and values historically associated with the Western political experience. The most prominent example of this defence was the Cold War itself – an ideological contest that shaped foreign and domestic policies, reorganized societies, and even modified the cultural attitudes of the time. Canada's foreign policy in the Cold War was an expression of its commitment to the Western ideals and principles that underpinned the post-1945 order. But Canada also participated in the Western alliance because of the promise of security and peace. As such, the postwar international system would be defended at all costs.

The Cold War gave credence to the neoclassical realist idea that system-level factors are critical to explaining how and why the politics of the era were modelled in specific ways.[1] Power and its distribution in the system, for example, privilege certain states and structure relations between them. But the use of power can also precipitate change; hence, the need to resist powerful states that would seek to revise the existing order. During the post-1945 era, the power struggle between the US and Soviet Union, in the latter's attempt to overturn the existing order, triggered a stalemate,

International Order and Canadian Aspirations 13

effectively deflecting the conflict and competition both outward toward the global periphery and into the realms of ideas, science, technology, and culture. This contest effectively shaped the international system and the very contours of political life at the time.

Although the historical bias inherent in the global order favoured the US, it continued to pursue several objectives that were in tension. In the shadow of the nuclear threat that characterized the Cold War, the US supported the status quo as the basis of a liberal peace while engaging the Soviet Union as a rival. In the context of this rivalry, the international system that was created – the Cold War system – tempered the behaviour of the two superpowers. A virtual stalemate, the Cold War system appeared immutable. History, however, reminds us that change is always possible. Indeed, formative historical processes – industrialization, urbanization, and globalization – as well as cataclysmic events have all been fundamental in altering past power balances. The weight of the US/USSR competition, and the latter's subsequent collapse, would serve as one such catalyst, formally bringing the Cold War era to a close.

As with all major shifts in the global balance of power, the fall of the Soviet Union created uncertainty while raising questions about how Canada and other countries tied to the order created in 1945 under US leadership would respond to this development. Despite the end of the Cold War, it soon became evident that the political impetus behind the original contest – defending the sphere of Western influence and control – remained, only with one key difference: there was now little opposition. As a result, a liberal expansionist agenda came to supplant the defensive posture historically associated with Cold War strategy and planning. However, it remained to be seen how the post-Soviet successor states would respond to this new development and what would be required to persuade and integrate these newly independent states into the liberal order.

As part of the coalition of states committed to the liberal international system, Canada looked to make a difference. It would do so in the context of its historical-cultural relationship with Ukraine by eliciting signals and soliciting commitments on such issues as nuclear disarmament. Meanwhile, by signalling its acceptance of the rules underpinning the existing order, Ukraine would in turn demonstrate its preparedness to join the coalition of states upholding the liberal order. This had a corresponding effect which intensified Canada's commitment to and relationship with Ukraine, linking the two nations' interests in unforeseen ways.

THE COLD WAR SYSTEM AND CANADIAN INTERESTS

As a foundation for international peace and security, the Western alliance recognized that support for the rules-based order was a political and moral necessity. This translated into a strong interest in defending the status quo. It was an impulse that ran deep, especially when the existing international order was threatened by states that would seek to overturn it using all the tools and methods at their disposal, including force. As Denis Stairs observed, states like Canada were committed to the existing order because they possessed "no interests that acquisitive acts of *dis*order can serve."[2] However, as a middle power, Canada was vulnerable. Therefore, Canada maintained a durable interest in lending its support to a stable, rules-based order, as doing so provided the most effective means of protecting its interests. This conservative approach to the country's interests – keeping that which it already possessed while supporting the right of other states to do the same – was reinforced throughout the Cold War, cementing Canada's position as an actor committed to defending the existing order: the status quo.[3]

Canada's reputation as a doggedly status quo power, however, was only partly explained by the types of benefits that would accrue to it under conditions of international peace and stability. Support was also extended because the basic design of the global system resonated with Canada's political culture. As such, since the system's inception in 1945, Canadian foreign policy makers viewed the maintenance of a rules-based order and the institutions supporting it as a first-order imperative. Throughout the Cold War, Conservative and Liberal prime ministers alike supported the North Atlantic Treaty Organization (NATO), the

United Nations (UN), the Group of Seven (G7), as well as other intergovernmental organizations. At first blush, this broad consensus suggests that Canada's foreign policy simply and more narrowly reflected Canadian strategic interests as a state committed to the status quo. But the post-1945 international order was also constructed in a manner that emphasized ideals associated with liberal democracy – political equality and rule of law, among others – and these, aligned as they were with Canada's political culture, increased its satisfaction with the system as constructed.

Not surprisingly, Canada's orientation placed it firmly within the Western camp. Moreover, a combination of domestic and international political factors precluded any significant departure from this coalition. Indeed, while the structure of the Cold War system and the specific configuration in the balance of power ruled out the possibility of Canadian neutrality, it was Canada's strong political, cultural, and historical ties to the United States and the United Kingdom as wartime allies that fixed its position within the transatlantic alliance. These shared principles, for which much was collectively sacrificed during the Second World War, reinforced the importance of this alliance in the public mind and gave it the appearance of being natural, rational, and right.

This commitment to Western liberal democratic values and principles was perhaps most clearly demonstrated by Canada's political elites, who unapologetically advocated for freedom and democracy throughout the Cold War. In the main, Canada's prime ministers – from Louis St Laurent to John Diefenbaker, to Lester Pearson, to Joe Clark, to Brian Mulroney – all viewed the Cold War in terms that extended well beyond its basic strategic dimension and significance. For these leaders, the Cold War represented the deeper struggle between open and closed political systems, the outcome of which would determine the future of the international order. Since Canada's leaders during this period viewed Western liberal values and principles – representative democracy and sovereign right, for example – as being far from inconsequential, they took the question of liberal democracy's immediate and future security as one of profound importance. Indeed, the coalition, especially in the form of NATO, offered

16 Canada and the Ukrainian Crisis

some assurance that the liberal ideals, which framed Western societies and ideologically underpinned the foundations of the world system (such as it was), would be preserved and protected.

For a middle power like Canada to be satisfied, however, it had to be assured not only that the international system reflected its political interests and values, but also that it was viable. Along with other coalition states, Canada would look to a system leader, or a state "that creates and maintains the global or regional hierarchy from which it accrues substantial benefits," to willingly shoulder the burden of defending the international system.[4] The system leader's role was to carry out the primary tasks associated with the defence of the system and to help guide a coalition of states that shared its interest in preserving the existing order. The acceptance of a system leader was predicated on its image and reputation as an actor that could, by virtue of its outsized power, effectively deter other malcontent states from pursuing ambitions that would seek to revise that order. The system leader would also function as a binding agent by instilling a sense of purpose and resolve within the coalition. In the post-1945 era, that system leader was the United States.

Fearing disorder and all it entailed, the coalition, under US guidance, would vigorously oppose any attempt by rival powers to revise the post-1945 order. The prevailing view and attitude at the time held that even small changes to the status quo had the potential to precipitate large and potentially unfavourable consequences. And although the transition from one order to the next could be peaceful, it could just as well devolve into a hegemonic war. Canada's enduring foreign policy alignment with the US-led coalition, therefore, reflected not only its satisfaction with the substance of the American-led order, but also the security benefits derived from it. This satisfaction was heightened by the lack of any other viable security arrangement.

At its core, the liberal order established after 1945 depended on the rules and institutions that defined it.[5] However, if the authority and integrity of these rules were to be maintained, US power and the political commitment of its leadership would be necessary. To this end, the United States was considered a vital actor prepared to enforce the order's foundational rules, since any significant decline in American power or commitment would have implied a weakening of the order it had originally authored.[6] Thus, the stability of the established order depended on the disposition of the system leader to use its power, often in the form of intervention.

Despite America's military and political might, the use of coercive power was not always reliable; encouragement and rewards often had the potential to be far more effective. In this regard, an important secondary objective was the integration of former adversaries and skeptics into the rules-based system.[7] This often took the form of persuasion. Characterized as a form of liberal hegemony that eschewed the formal aspects of imperial rule in favour of political influence and control, this type of global leadership necessarily favoured assistance initiatives.[8] As such, support for democratic institution building as well as economic assistance and development aid became the primary mechanisms through which the US and its allies tried to convince adversaries and ambivalent countries alike to accept the principles underpinning a rules-based order. This project, however, was also contingent on the strength of the coalition's commitment to its ideological objectives. The alliance had to demonstrate an unwavering commitment to the liberal order and a willingness to fight, if necessary, to preserve the order's basic political character.

While Canada and its allies would retain a critical interest in preserving the post-1945 order, separately they did not possess the resources required to do so.[9] As a result, Canada and the other coalition members would come to depend upon the power and leadership of the United States. In turn, however, despite its military pre-eminence and prowess, the US would depend on the support of its allies, including Canada, to fulfil its duties as system leader, since it too did not entirely possess the political or military resources sufficient to achieve unchecked dominance on its own. Thus, the US looked to a coalition to assist with the provision of international goods, such as security, prosperity, and stability, in both the developing and (after 1989) transitioning worlds.[10] America's allies viewed this type of assistance as a strategic imperative. For its part, Canada would come to accept a closer working relationship with the US as system leader.

Canada's tendency to align its policies with those of the US was most pronounced in its security policy. As a founding member of NATO, Canada had shown itself to be a staunch supporter of the Western alliance. While NATO was a key component in the West's security architecture, its ultimate purpose was to "unify satisfied nations under the leadership of the dominant nation."[11] To this end, the strongest signal of Canada's commitment to the US-led coalition was, in fact, its membership within this organization. Canada would demonstrate the depth of this commitment by expending significant resources in support of NATO missions throughout the Cold War. This commitment reflected both Canada's interest in system stability and its adherence to the set of guiding liberal and democratic principles that had bound the alliance since its inception.[12]

With US leadership on offer, the Canadian effort to achieve its desired objectives by following the American lead sometimes entailed the adoption of measures that mirrored US strategy. In this way, Canada, along with other NATO allies, demonstrated a historical willingness to help augment and even compensate for the gaps in America's capacity to project power. Thus, Canada joined the US and other key Western allies in the Korean War, maintained a force presence in Europe throughout the Cold War, and, in general, nurtured a close defence alliance and political relationship with the United States. For members of the coalition, support required not only acquiescing to the system leader's policies, but also participating actively in carrying out its strategic agenda through internationally sanctioned means. Consequently, the essence of following the US during this period was to mimic its behaviour in relation to issues of shared importance.

Indeed, during the Cold War, Canada's foreign policy often reflected US concerns and priorities, pointing to an enduring alignment of interests and values between the two states. While principled differences did exist between the two countries – a function of domestic considerations and different leadership priorities and styles – Canada possessed a strong interest in echoing if not endorsing the American position on matters pertaining to system stability and risk mitigation. Even leaders such as Pierre Elliott Trudeau, who chafed at the idea of American leadership, understood the importance of maintaining a unified front in the face of the threat posed by the USSR. No less important, tending to this imperative limited Canada's foreign policy independence. Refusal to support a major American-led initiative had the potential of jeopardizing Canada's influence in Washington (where it mattered most), leaving it vulnerable to various forms of censure.[13] Furthermore, while important policy differences existed between Canada and the US during the Cold War – Cuba, Vietnam, and the installation of nuclear weapons on Canadian soil, for instance – Canadian officials understood that Canada had a greater opportunity to affect outcomes from within a US-led coalition. This realization would prove significant. Maximizing Canadian influence would later become increasingly important, especially at times when the international order was at stake and Canada's doubts about the wisdom of US actions appeared well founded.

Yet, to fully appreciate Canada's interest in preserving the existing order, the following counterfactual needs to be considered. The absence or retreat of a rules-based order carried with it the prospect of widespread uncertainty and distrust between state actors, with the potential to spark new regional security competitions or reinvigorate old ones. Aside from leaving Canada more vulnerable and dependent on a less constrained US, the collapse of the Cold War system – despite its apparent limitations and risks – would have also brought with it other, potentially dire consequences. The chaos that might have been unleashed could very well have embroiled Canada in new military conflicts on an unprecedented scale. Being involved in two world wars during the twentieth century had made painfully clear to Canada the strategic necessity of taking proactive steps toward maintaining international stability.

The Cold War not only established the parameters of Canada's foreign policy but also shaped the very content of the decisions taken. The US-led coalition responded to the requirements associated with maintaining international stability, which necessarily privileged the status quo. Brought together by their shared interest in the existing order and the ideas and principles that guided it, these states would demonstrate their resolve in defending the prevailing order on numerous occasions throughout the Cold War. This was no small matter, as nothing less than its defence would do. But it was also the case that every decision and action would be filtered through the lens of maintaining a favourable balance of power. There could be no deviation from this objective, if only because it spoke to the overarching principle that governed modern statecraft – state survival. Ultimately, the coalition sought to ensure the preservation of the existing order, but it also remained mindful of the possibility of change, and of the challenges and opportunities that would be presented if that came to pass.

SOVIET COLLAPSE AND CANADA'S DEVELOPING INTEREST IN UKRAINE

Several important developments shaped the trajectory of East-West relations in the lead-up to the collapse of the Soviet Union. As the USSR embarked on a program of reform (*perestroika*) and openness (*glasnost*) under Soviet General Secretary Mikhail Gorbachev, it began to respond more favourably to Western engagement. This was a significant development, which signalled the emergence of an unprecedented opportunity for the West to curtail the Soviet Union's longstanding revisionist aspirations. According to Schweller and Wohlforth, "the status quo powers [viewed] détente not simply as a process codifying the rules of the game to regulate further competition but rather as a means to convert the dissatisfied power into a status quo one."[14] This courtship was now possible because the worsening economic situation created by the weight of the contradictions resulting from Mikhail Gorbachev's reforms had stripped the USSR of the requisite power to pursue its historical ambition of overturning the liberal order. With the goals of expansion and global revolution beyond reach, Soviet officials pursued the more modest objective of simply maintaining the assets and resources already under their control.[15] This dramatic shift in strategic thinking

International Order and Canadian Aspirations   21

resulted in the USSR embracing the status quo. Meanwhile, the United States would accept no less. As outlined in National Security Directive 23 (NSD 23), the US adopted a bold, new posture in its engagement with the USSR, seeking to integrate it within the existing international framework.[16]

In the waning years of the USSR's existence, Soviet acceptance of the American and thus the coalition's understanding of the nature of their relationship resulted in what has been described as "the intellectual capitulation of the weaker side to the stronger."[17] After the collapse of the USSR, this understanding would shape the pattern of engagement between the West and the post-Soviet successor states. It reflected the coalition's confidence in the superiority of the liberal political-economic model while clearly signalling the strength of the American-led order. However, the demise of the Soviet Union did not represent the triumph of liberalism or the "end of history" as some had predicted.[18] Rather, the occasion replaced an old challenge – the struggle between competing ideologies – with a new one: uncertainty and insecurity in Central and Eastern Europe, with the potential for chaos.

Nevertheless, for Canada, several constants remained. Strengthened by the additional security benefits derived from the end of the Cold War and American hegemony, Canada's interest in a rules-based order remained unshakable. And while many of the constraints that were associated with the balance of power had disappeared, its foreign policy remained oriented toward the pursuit of stability. Yet, now unfettered, Canada and its coalition allies were better positioned to pursue this interest through more innovative security policies. Indeed, with the Soviet Union gone and the liberal international order secure against any immediate challenger, Canada and other coalition states under American leadership shifted their attention away from system defence. Their focus was directed instead at consolidating the security gains that had resulted from the Cold War's end.

It was within this evolving political environment that the Canadian government, under Brian Mulroney, embraced an interventionist foreign policy ethic that placed greater strategic emphasis on promoting a liberal global agenda. This shift reflected his government's ideological commitment to the strategic dissemination of Western liberal values. It also reflected the loosening of the Cold War constraints that had lessened the costs associated with pursuing a more interventionist strategy. Thus, a combination of internal and external factors heightened Canadian confidence in the Western developmental model as the vehicle by which political, social, and economic progress could be achieved internationally. From the outset, the Mulroney government adopted a good governance policy that was consistent with the spirit of these goals as part of the effort to promote democratic development and human rights abroad.[19]

This policy represented a significant shift in Canada's stance on sovereignty-related international norms, focusing on "how states governed their societies and on the right of external agents – governments, non-governmental organizations, and multilateral institutions – to intervene to protect or restore specific political and economic practices."[20] Moreover, the policy brought Canada closer in line with America's newly emboldened post–Cold War agenda, which sought to spread democratic and free-market principles abroad.[21] Meanwhile, the Mulroney government's new interest in the governance performance of states coincided with Canada's engagement with Ukraine, which had gained its independence through a plebiscite on 1 December 1991. Just as US policy aimed to transform the entire post-Soviet sphere, Canada's good governance policy was geared toward encouraging a similar development in relation to Ukraine, with which Canada enjoyed close ties because of enduring historical-cultural links.

Security, nonetheless, consisted of more than the advantage of pressing home the importance of good governance. The coalition's strong interest in converting the former Soviet republics into reliable partners compelled them to identify and interpret the intentions of the actors emerging from the post-Soviet space.[22] Did these states still harbour ambitions or favour policies that might otherwise undermine system stability? Consequently, following the collapse of the USSR, the goal of Canada's early foreign policy engagement with Ukraine (and the coalition's engagement more generally) was to clarify whether and to what extent the latter accepted the legitimacy of the existing international order.[23] The answers to these questions would guide both the nature and scope of Canada's interests in Ukraine and the range of practical options the government would choose in pursuing and advancing those interests. This determination was especially critical in the case of Ukraine, since it had gained its independence while still in possession of a large share of the Soviet nuclear arsenal. There was, however, a lingering problem: how were policy makers to distinguish between states with exploitative preferences and those emergent states with defensive intentions?[24]

The unravelling of the Soviet Union was accompanied by considerable uncertainty. Despite the impressive results of Ukraine's independence referendum, its claim to sovereignty was contested. Statements emanating from Moscow questioning Ukraine's right to self-determination were worrisome. Predictably, Ukraine clung to the nuclear weapons on its territory, a move that was initially difficult to interpret. Some viewed this as a defensive measure. Others chalked it up to obstinate behaviour. Nevertheless, international security depended on nuclear non-proliferation and thus Ukraine's actions could not be easily countenanced.[25] Indeed, for Canada and the coalition, foreign policy pivoted on whether the liberal rules-based order would be accepted or rejected. Ultimately, Ukraine's decision regarding denuclearization would determine the course of its relationship with Canada in particular and the West more generally.[26]

Confronted by the possibility of international isolation and sanctions, Ukraine agreed to relinquish control over the weapons on its territory in exchange for a security guarantee by the major powers in the form of the Budapest Memorandum.[27] Given that Canada's focus on Ukraine's nuclear intentions was largely aimed at determining its orientation toward the liberal order, the Ukrainian response of adhering to the Nuclear Non-Proliferation Treaty represented a necessary first-step, signalling that it could be persuaded to accept the basic tenets of the order that Canada insisted on.

The dissolution of the USSR presented the coalition with a unique historical opportunity to enhance the stability of the

American-led order by eliciting signals. Furthermore, the need to access Western capital, technical assistance, and expertise among these newly independent states, including Ukraine, enhanced the bargaining position of middle powers such as Canada.[28] Among Ukrainians, it was expected that good relations with countries like Canada would lead to greater opportunities for economic growth and political legitimacy. But, more to the point, Ukraine and the other successor states were persuaded to emulate the Western developmental model because under the circumstances it was the only available avenue toward possible economic recovery and stability.

While other post-Soviet states shared a similar interest, Ukraine, relatively speaking, was better positioned than most to make rapid progress. With its resources, human capital, and industrial base, the future for Ukraine seemed most promising. From the perspective of the coalition states, Ukraine's emergence as a prosperous and even secure democracy offered potentially significant benefits as well. In expanding the global zone of democracies, the US-led coalition could further consolidate the security gains that had resulted from the end of the Cold War while reasserting the Western developmental model's wider relevance. In this sense, Ukraine was viewed as an important litmus test.

Within Canadian circles, this apparent potential fostered the belief that Canada could reap quick political dividends by assisting Ukraine. However, this belief was predicated on the idea that Canada's large Ukrainian diaspora, with its interest in their ancestral land, would play a role. It was expected that the government's aid to Ukraine would be augmented by the contributions of Ukrainian Canadians, as government officials projected such combined investments would yield greater strategic dividends than sole-purposed assistance to other politically and economically disadvantaged countries.

The similarity of interests that existed between the government and the Ukrainian-Canadian community necessarily worked to the advantage of each. By staking out complementary positions on expanding Canada's engagement with Ukraine, both parties were set to cooperate. Curiously, this cooperation was viewed as evidence of the community's influence over the Canadian government's foreign policy. It was an assessment, however, that failed to recognize the role that mutual gain would play, which necessarily animated and informed the spirit of the relationship. Indeed, in the case of the Mulroney government, the strategic cooperation that took place with the community elevated expectations regarding the potential effectiveness of Canadian aid to Ukraine and boosted Canada's confidence in the superiority of the liberal developmental model. It also provided Canada with leverage that could be used to obtain even clearer signals of Ukraine's commitment to institutionalized rules and norms. Meanwhile, reinforcing the community's commitment to cooperate with the government in its strategic goals and priorities necessarily gave Canada the incentive to stand by Ukraine in the following years despite Ukraine's uneven progress on reforms.

In the end, however, whether it was the Mulroney, Chrétien, or Martin government, Canadian engagement was ultimately contingent on Ukraine's willingness to signal its acceptance of the bedrock rules and norms of the post–Cold War international order.[29] Canada's attempts to solicit such commitments spoke to its interest in acquiring credible information about the Ukrainian government's intentions, since this played an important role in shaping Canada's international priorities. While Ukraine's fate had strategic implications for the stability of the existing order, Canada could not afford to expend its resources in pursuit of unrealistic objectives. If Canadian officials had concluded that Ukraine was unlikely to adhere to norms such as nuclear nonproliferation or had no intention of pursuing the domestic reforms that Canada deemed necessary, its engagement priorities would have shifted in an entirely different direction. Canadian interest in Ukraine's successful transition, and the significant resources allocated to this end, could not have been justified without a reasonable expectation of success.

The interest that successor states like Ukraine demonstrated in the Western model no doubt reinforced the view of Brian Mulroney – and of the other prime ministers to follow – that Canada could and, indeed, *should* play a role in guiding the country's political and economic future. Together, Ukrainian interest and Canadian confidence provided the impetus for the sort of engagement that came to define, in part, the special nature of the relationship. This enhanced interest in Canada-Ukraine relations was preceded by changes in the international system that created conditions enabling Canada to project its values abroad. However, it was the willingness of successive Canadian governments to chart this course, and to remain true in their wider strategic commitment to Western liberal ideals and geopolitical objectives, that ultimately gave new meaning to Canada's relations with Ukraine in the immediate post–Cold War period.

CONCLUSION

During the Cold War, all aspects of political life fell under the spell of the superpower rivalry. This decades-long impasse divided and mobilized humanity on a massive scale, defined the interests of states, and dictated the decisions of foreign policy makers. The conflict appeared to validate the notion that the Cold War system shaped reality itself. This was largely attributable to the central role that the two vastly different and competing ideologies had in determining how political, social, and economic life should be organized. Given the stakes involved, states and societies mobilized a considerable share of their resources in support of this competitive effort. As such, how the conflict ended came as a complete surprise. There was no crowning finale and no gleeful satisfaction. The Cold War was simply over.

Yet, the end of the Cold War did not mean an end to the ambitions of liberal hegemony. The imperative associated with defending the liberal democratic order basically shifted toward its consolidation and expansion. The collapse of the Soviet Union had removed a key barrier. Still, the newly independent states of the former USSR faced enormous challenges that potentially hindered their seamless transition into the post–Cold War international system. Ukraine's failure to make this transition quickly would pose a particular risk given the legacy of its Soviet-era nuclear arsenal. Its successful conversion, on the other hand,

International Order and Canadian Aspirations

presented coalition states, including Canada, with an opportunity to expand the zone of democracies and strengthen international security.[30] Thus, Ukraine emerged as a keystone in the effort to consolidate the post–Cold War order.

Canada made Ukraine a priority from the outset. Yet, the relationship was a tentative one. Although Ottawa managed initially to leverage its influence – successfully eliciting institutional signals from Ukraine on nuclear disarmament – the degree of Ukrainian follow-through on reforms left something to be desired. Nevertheless, Canada would stay the course, seeking more and deeper commitments. This persistence reflected Canada's confidence in the Western liberal democratic project and enduring interest in providing Ukraine with a map to guide its eventual transformation into a successful status quo state. To this end, Canada supplied Ukraine with various forms of development assistance – especially when doing so helped Ukraine to fulfill its international and bilateral commitments. Along the way, an anxious Ukrainian-Canadian community earnestly looked to work with a government that was similarly inclined, laying down the foundations for a cooperative relationship.

Ultimately, however, if Canada's interests were to be satisfied, Ukraine had to adhere to liberal democratic values and meet its responsibilities as a member of the international community. These considerations played a significant part in shaping and lending a special quality to Canada's relationship with Ukraine, enabling Canada to serve as a mentor to the latter along its path toward acceptance, security, and prosperity. Still, Canada's motives were not entirely altruistic. By assisting Ukraine, Canada was fulfilling its obligations with regard to fortifying and expanding the rules-based order and US-led coalition to which it remained committed since 1945 and in which it had a vested interest.

2

The Ukrainian Crisis, Canada, and World Order: Systemic Imperatives and the Canadian Response

Neoclassical realism acknowledges that the structure of an international order rests on the distribution of power within the system, engendering both constraint and incentive for states operating within it.[1] A stable order favours constraint, generating as it does a bias toward upholding the status quo, since a significant shift in the balance of power can destabilize an order to a dangerous extent and even precipitate its collapse. Status quo actors, therefore, have an enormous interest in maintaining a favourable balance of power so as to limit challenges to the order as constructed. Yet, for dissatisfied states, a change in the distribution of power is regarded as an opportunity to revise the status quo at the expense of the satisfied powers. For such states, change is not only welcomed but also encouraged. Given this tension, there is considerable fertile ground for a high-stakes competition to occur between satisfied and dissatisfied states.

In the initial post–Cold War years, the balance of power tilted heavily in favour of the United States, with many states accepting its political leadership. The first Gulf War was an example of its dominance. In due course, however, there was evidence that the balance of power was shifting. The retrenchment in US global influence and power – the result of its involvement in prolonged and costly wars in Afghanistan and Iraq – signalled potential instability within the system. Responding to this opportunity, an assertive and resurgent Russia would challenge the existing order.

Beginning in earnest with Russia's war with Georgia in 2008, the trend accelerated in 2014, when, despite its denials, Russia invaded Ukraine. Russia's actions were widely regarded as an ominous sign. Whatever was left of the optimism and cooperation that had defined the early post–Cold War period quickly vanished. The international system had entered a period of precipitous decline, creating a crisis of confidence that would reshape Canadian foreign policy.

Russia's challenge to the post–Cold War order introduced a dangerous dynamic within the system, which became manifest in the form of the Ukrainian crisis. Moreover, Russia's willingness to use military force to seize and annex the territory of its neighbour was indicative of its resolve. No other state was so fully committed to the project of revising the status quo. More to the point, Russia's actions flagrantly contravened the very rules and norms that helped minimize the chances of a general conflict throughout the Cold War and early post–Cold War periods. At its core, the renewed competition between Western and Russian visions of world order mirrored the newly invigorated competition between liberal and illiberal ideas. The triumph of liberalism no longer seemed as inevitable as it had at the start of the post–Cold War period, when Russia agreed to observe the principles and norms governing the international system.

The Ukrainian crisis signalled the denouement of the post–Cold War era. Indeed, Russia's renewed challenge alerted Western leaders to the fact it was no longer a foregone conclusion that the international order would continue to function as designed. Given the nature of Russia's challenge, the stakes could not have been higher for status quo states like Canada. Global change would once again alter the international power dynamic, and Canada's response would depend on its perception of what the Ukrainian crisis meant for world order and how best to cope with it.

THE INTERNATIONAL ORDER IN CRISIS

Lacking the necessary resources to challenge the emergent post–Cold War order, Russia inherited the USSR's quiescent foreign policy orientation in 1991. This orientation resulted from the myriad difficulties that followed the USSR's collapse, which significantly constrained Russia's capabilities throughout the 1990s.[2] Forced to adapt to the new limits on its power, Russia would comply with many of the rules and norms of the international system. For a time, even, Russia's participation in key institutions as a full-fledged member created the impression that it acknowledged the system's legitimacy. This period of transition, however, was also one of great domestic disorder and upheaval in Russia. Attributed to policy drift, the disarray that accompanied this shift had to be addressed if the country was to recover its previous standing and influence.

Following the turbulence associated with the presidency of Boris Yeltsin, the consolidation of power under Russia's new president, Vladimir Putin, and the reversal of its economic slide through the exploitation of newfound energy reserves, would eventually pave the way for Russia's return to international prominence.[3] Once its military and intelligence capabilities were rebuilt, Russia grew more assertive in the first decade of the new millennium. It attempted, for example, to restore an exclusive sphere of influence over the former Soviet republics – the so-called "near abroad." This resulted in a series of conflicts and secessionist movements in the periphery of the former USSR: Artsakh (Azerbaijan), Transnistria (Moldova), and Abkhazia and South Ossetia (Georgia). No longer committed to the international order as constructed, Russia quickly asserted itself as a limited-aims revisionist power.[4]

The new direction in Russia's foreign policy would have mattered less were it not for the opportunities that resulted from US retrenchment. After nearly a decade at war, the United States had grown weary of costly entanglements abroad. Moreover, the burden of America's global leadership had given rise to domestic partisan disputes, impeding its activity on the international stage and causing it to be more reserved in its actions. America's cautious approach to Libya's civil conflict in 2011 and its reluctance to involve itself in Syria's internationalized civil war would underscore this point. Meanwhile, Washington's reticence did not go

The Ukrainian Crisis, Canada, and World Order   31

unnoticed, signalling to its allies that robust American leadership was no longer guaranteed. The US retreat brought with it unanticipated consequences for international peace and security, the most significant being the creation of space in which other actors could operate.

The question of whether the US remained willing to carry out the full spectrum of its duties as system leader was of importance to the coalition, as the order's stability could only be assured if the system leader's commitment remained firm. Potential aggressors had to be deterred by the reasonable expectation that a US-led coalition would enforce the rules and punish offenders if necessary. Indeed, a dissatisfied state that harboured aggressive intentions was more likely to wage war if it expected not to be confronted for its actions. More importantly, however, member states of the coalition would have been forced to re-evaluate many of their core assumptions about defence if US security commitments were no longer regarded as reliable.

America's failure to enforce a red line on Syrian chemical weapons in 2013 was precisely the sort of development that undermined its credibility as system leader. However, it was the implications of this action that registered most with allies. According to French President François Hollande, America's restraint altered Vladimir Putin's assessment of the strategic landscape and encouraged Russia's aggression against Ukraine. On this point, the French president was unequivocal. The American reluctance to deal decisively with Bashar al-Assad's use of chemical weapons against Syrian opposition strongholds "was interpreted as weakness from the international community." This, Hollande bluntly concluded, "provoked the crisis in Ukraine, the illegal annexation of Crimea, and what's happening in Syria right now."[5] US reticence thus introduced doubt about the strength of its resolve to uphold the existing order. The gap between the vigorous language used by American officials to affirm their commitment to maintaining the status quo and their unwillingness to act toward this end consequently emboldened Vladimir Putin to test America's – and, by extension, the coalition's – commitment to Ukraine.

Russia's annexation of Crimea in 2014 marked a turning point in post–Cold War relations. For the first time in Europe since the Second World War, a state had forcibly seized and annexed the territory of its neighbour, thus contravening a host of international agreements and multilateral commitments, including the UN Charter, the CSCE Final Act, and the Budapest Memorandum of 1994.[6] By engaging in predatory behaviour and violating key rules and norms embedded in the international order, Russia abrogated its international obligations, effectively placing the post–Cold War settlement in doubt. Indeed, norms that prohibited forcible territorial expansion were considered inviolate throughout the post-1945 period, and states that did not follow these standards were severely punished. Iraq's invasion of Kuwait served as one of the principal drivers behind the 1991 Gulf War.[7] Yet, unlike Iraq, Russia possessed great-power status, permanent membership on the UN Security Council, and nuclear weapons. As such, Russia's violation of the foundational rules of the international order posed a far greater challenge to global peace and security than had Saddam Hussein's invasion and annexation of Kuwait. Moreover, Russia's challenge could not be addressed simply by military means. An armed response had the potential to escalate the conflict significantly with unforeseen and possibly catastrophic results.

While such dangers all but precluded US-led military intervention to restore the territorial integrity of Ukraine in 2014, Russia's actions could not be allowed to stand. The coalition, as a result, adopted a long-term, non-kinetic approach that relied mainly on the imposition of economic sanctions against Russia as punishment for its violations. Although this approach was carefully selected to minimize the possibility of blowback, it still carried risks. If the coalition's strategy proved ineffective, its leverage over Russia would be reduced, complicating further efforts in addressing future non-compliance.[8] The strategy also had the potential of hastening a strategic realignment between Moscow and Beijing that would have altered the balance of power between revisionist and conservative powers, opening the door to a powerful coalition of dissatisfied states.[9] Such a development would have advantaged revisionist forces worldwide and signalled an even more precipitous decline in the stability of the existing international order. Despite the seriousness of these concerns, as things stood the risks associated with doing nothing were even greater.

US retrenchment and Russian non-compliance together provided evidence of an increasingly unstable system.[10] This led to growing recognition among alliance members, including Canada, of their responsibility toward offsetting the risks associated with US retrenchment. While the existing order's long-term viability ultimately depended upon US power, the support of the coalition was needed to help counteract the destabilizing effects of America's retreat. The alliance would achieve this partly by assuming a greater share of the burden involved in maintaining the coalition's deterrence capabilities. Therefore, in addition to fully supporting the sanctions regime imposed upon Russia, coalition states, including Canada, would deploy trainers and advisers to help Ukraine enhance its military effectiveness. It would also participate in a NATO mission to shore up Europe's eastern defences in Poland, the Baltics, and the Black Sea, deploying joint air, sea, and land task forces.[11]

The willingness of the coalition to engage actively in this overall effort was seen as vital to international security. Indeed, the success of the strategy depended on cooperation to a larger extent than it would have if a simple kinetic response were viable. In its encumbered state, the US would have found it difficult on its own to compel Russia to alter its behaviour. A unified coalition, in contrast, could exact much greater costs. No less important was the fact that, while the coalition's support had earlier served mainly to legitimate US military aims and actions during the first Gulf War, cooperation in dealing with the Russian threat would demonstrate a collective commitment to global security. Peace and order could only be achieved through combined action. The decision to work together clarified the stakes involved while emphasizing that there was no alternative to cooperation if peace and the restoration of the status quo were the desired goals. In this regard, the decision to mobilize a broad-based coalition was rooted in necessity, not just strategic preference.

The US recognized the situational importance of encouraging cooperation and, to a large degree, American leadership enabled and actively facilitated this objective.[12] Occasionally, however, certain non-systemic factors complicated this aim. The US could lead only to the extent that others were willing to follow. This willingness had been seriously undercut by George W. Bush's 2003 decision to pursue regime change in Iraq. The second Gulf War, with its suspect pretext for going to war (weapons of mass destruction), diminished US global leadership. In the run-up to the Iraq invasion, Germany, for example, with its sensitivity to domestic opposition constituencies, was wary of being drawn into what were described as dubious "adventures."[13] In Canada, similar conditions applied, with public opinion firmly against war.[14] This pointed to a discernible truth: the pressure exercised by citizens could not be entirely ignored, underscoring the tension that exists between priorities at the domestic and international levels.[15] The crusading nature of US foreign policy served as a sober reminder of the need to be cautious, and public opinion acted as an important brake on the impulse to follow. Nevertheless, 2003 was not 2014.

Indeed, during the Ukrainian crisis, the ability of the coalition members to overcome the weight of these and other domestic considerations reflected the degree of clarity that existed around the stakes involved. This understanding would compel alliance partners to respond in a manner consistent with their respective security interests and obligations, and shape the mindset of foreign policy makers while tempering their inclination to pursue other goals. Faced with an international crisis, pragmatic leaders, including Canada's Prime Minister Stephen Harper, would all come to recognize the principal importance of prioritizing a policy that focused on shoring up system stability – a first-order imperative – rather than simply tending to domestic concerns or yielding to public opinion and pressure.

As Harper told the crew of HMCS *Fredericton*, while aboard the frigate in the Baltic Sea as part of the NATO mission, "Mr. Putin's recklessness threatens global stability, regional stability, and has spread fear among our eastern allies. That, my

The Ukrainian Crisis, Canada, and World Order 35

friends, is why you, the men and women of the Royal Canadian Navy, are here."[16] Contributing to the defence of Eastern Europe and the alliance mission in Ukraine, he stated, was Canada's answer to Russia's breach of the international rules. In doing so, those states that were most vulnerable would be assured that they were not alone. Offering words of encouragement, he added, "stand[ing] up for what is right and good in our troubled world," the prime minister declared, "is what Canadians naturally did and would continue to do." Considering the strategic nature of the threat, however, he might easily have said that doing nothing was not an option.

SYSTEM STABILITY, THE UKRAINIAN CRISIS, AND CANADA

The Harper government's response to Russia's challenge consisted of two main elements. First, Canada lent its support to US-backed measures designed to impose costs on Russia for contravening international norms and violating the existing rules. These measures were intended to contain and ultimately reverse Russian behaviour. Second, Canada increased its support for Ukraine in order to manage the effects of Russia's actions. Both elements were related to system defence, with the imperative to follow the system leader becoming an even greater strategic concern than usual.

By way of contrast, not all coalition states looked to commit with the same sense of urgency as the Harper government.[17] Nominally, the influence of domestic public opinion produced countervailing pressures that led to reticence among certain states. However, even they would ultimately follow, if only because the efficacy of the coalition's response depended upon enacting sanctions on a unanimous basis.[18] The coalition members were fully aware that undermining the sanctions regime would raise doubts about the coalition's resolve, thereby weakening its deterrence capabilities. The potential risks of a timid response would only have increased in view of both America's retrenchment and the turmoil roiling the European Union in

2014 – the Greek financial crisis, disputes over refugees and migration controls, and talk of Brexit.

Given these situational imperatives, Canada therefore sought to strengthen the coalition's unity and resolve by making evident the acute nature of the threat. Specifically, the Harper government highlighted Russia's strategy of disinformation, questioning its credibility and commitment to international peace and security. Foremost, Harper rejected both Russia's characterization of the crisis in Ukraine as a political coup and the rationale behind its actions.[19] He also pushed back when the passenger aircraft Malaysia Airlines flight MH17 was downed by a surface-to-air missile launched from a Russian missile battery in insurgent-controlled territory, claiming 298 civilian lives. Responding to the Kremlin narrative, which denied all knowledge of the incident and asserted that Ukraine was responsible for any and all occurrences on its territory, Harper averred, "while we do not know who is responsible for this attack, we continue to condemn Russia's military aggression and illegal occupation of Ukraine, which is at the root of the ongoing conflict in the region."[20] Pledging Canada's support for an independent international investigation, the prime minister was unequivocal in his contention that those responsible would be held to account. As for the continued prevarication of the Russian government denying involvement (despite mounting evidence that the missile launcher was part of Russia's 53rd Anti-Aircraft Missile Brigade), he declared, "the only truth we can be certain of in any statement coming out of the Putin regime is that the truth must be something else entirely."[21]

The prime minister's statement was a rejection of Russia's characterization of its role. But the statement also focused attention on Russia's reliability writ large. The rules-based order hinged on the obligations of states to abide by agreements. The Budapest Memorandum, to which Russia was a signatory, guaranteed Ukraine's sovereignty. Thus, Russia's abrogation of its obligations under the agreement not only served to destabilize the existing order but also cast doubt on the sincerity of any future assurances. The Harper government was adamant that, by breaching the rules, norms, and its commitments, Russia had become a strategic adversary. Consequently, the only way to persuade Russia to accept its international responsibilities was for the coalition to stand firm in the face of the violations.[22]

Ottawa's position echoed the American concern that Russia represented a strategic threat by jeopardizing the principles and ideals that made international stability possible.[23] Speaking before a gathering of the NATO Council of Canada, Canada's foreign minister, John Baird, articulated the government's understanding of the wider stakes involved. According to Baird, the crisis was not simply about Ukraine. Rather, he explained, Russia's actions had undermined "the very foundations of our rules-based international system." In frank terms, Baird proceeded to lay out the potential consequences of a declining order: "The absence of rules and of trust, compounded by aggression founded on deception, erodes stability and leads to chaos."[24] Although Baird's allusion to the potential dangers of second- and third-order effects that could follow from acts of disorder was meant to be cautionary, it was also in keeping with Canada's orthodox perspective on the global order and its implications for Canadian strategic interests. Accordingly, the Harper government's support for the US as system leader was considered vital, its endorsement of the American interpretation of the crisis following directly from its position on global stability.[25]

The government's support for the US, however, was also buttressed by its criticism of Russia's interpretation of the source of the conflict as Western-inspired.[26] In late 2014, Baird took the unusual step of writing an op-ed piece, which appeared in the *Toronto Star* and sought publicly to frame and explain the crisis and Canada's assessment of the situation. The Canadian foreign minister specifically cited the ways in which Russia's aggression ran contrary to Russian interests, contributing to its growing international isolation. In Baird's view, the foreign policy of President Putin risked making "the historical fear of encirclement a self-fulfilling prophecy, by turning friends into adversaries."[27] But by explicitly rejecting Moscow's characterization of the crisis as a Western-instigated coup, Baird also challenged Russia's justification of its actions in Ukraine. In his view, Russia's behaviour made it culpable. It alone was responsible for the crisis, and the resolution of the crisis would only occur when Russia abandoned its wayward behaviour and accepted the norms and principles of the governing system, including recognizing Ukraine's sovereignty by withdrawing from Crimea. The failure to do so would entail additional costs.

Baird, however, was no less clear that these consequences were the result of misguided leadership. For Baird, ever careful to make a clear distinction between Russia's government and its people, Vladimir Putin was at the centre of the country's troubles. Putin had "hijack[ed] the narrative and fram[ed] relationships in adversarial terms for both domestic and international purposes," the foreign minister argued, preventing Russia from achieving "a prominent place in today's international order."[28] The global community, according to Baird, could not afford to be complacent. "There cannot be business as usual," the foreign minister declared, "between Russia and the international community."[29] In this regard, the international community, collectively, needed to pressure Russia, especially its leadership. To this end, the Harper government welcomed the growing sanctions employed not only against entities (banks, oil-and-gas corporations, and military enterprises) but also individuals directly involved in leading Russia's policy of aggression. Barred from international economic dealings and proscribed in their freedom to travel for having flouted international rules, the intent was to make clear that those responsible would be held personally to account for their actions.

Canada's tough talk and support for sanctions, however, had to be interpreted against the backdrop of the strength and motivation behind its relations with Ukraine since that country's independence. A key objective of Canada's longstanding Ukraine strategy was to help the country achieve economic growth and better governance. Since other countries were in similar need of assistance, this objective only partly explains why Canada prioritized the relationship. What mattered was that a stable and prosperous Ukraine was likely to be a strong supporter of the coalition and would contribute positively to peace and international security. An unstable Ukraine, on the other hand, could become a source of further conflict and uncertainty. No less important, it was in Canada's and the alliance's interests to have Ukraine as a coalition member due to its abundance of natural and human resources. The addition of Ukraine's military, even in its degraded condition, would increase the alliance's defence capabilities and, conversely, impede Russia from adding to its power, thereby averting an even greater challenge and threat to the post–Cold War order.[30] By assisting Ukraine in its reforms and aiding the country where it could, the alliance would create a bulwark against Russian expansionism while improving its own security.

Nonetheless, there were limits to what Canada could or would do. While the alliance maintained a strong interest in strengthening the Ukrainian state as a way to deter Russia from seizing even more territory, it was reluctant to provide lethal military assistance. Under President Barack Obama, Washington argued that supplying advanced weapons systems would fail to improve Ukraine's overall strategic position. While lethal military assistance would have enhanced Ukrainian security in the mid- to long term, Washington reasoned that Ukraine's capacity to capitalize on those gains in the short term was less certain and even possibly counterproductive. Ukraine's security would be better served by the success of its domestic reforms. That the US did not wish to give Russia any opportunity to recast the conflict as a proxy war was, of course, an additional factor.

Despite its global leadership role, US reticence compelled the Ukrainian government to lobby Canada and several other NATO countries for advanced weapons. However, these entreaties were roundly rejected. For the Harper government, its reluctance stemmed not simply from a fear of escalation (although this too was a concern); rather, its refusal to provide lethal military aid was more directly governed by the US position on the issue. Jason Kenney, speaking in his capacity as minister of defence, stated: "We continue to review the possibility of providing lethal defensive equipment, but Canada will not act alone in this respect."[31] The limits imposed on Canada by American global leadership mattered. With its focus on balancing system requirements, Washington would steer the coalition's strategic approach. Until a different strategy materialized, Canada would follow suit (as it traditionally did), providing only non-lethal military assistance while expanding support for reforms in Ukraine.[32]

The Ukrainian Canadian Congress (UCC) understood these constraints. Russia had the capacity and the will to ratchet up its support for the insurgents in the Donbas and increase its own involvement in the conflict if it chose to do so. The presence of tens of thousands of Russian troops on Ukraine's border was deliberate in this regard, and would give pause to the Western allies in their response. Yet, as the UCC national executive noted on several occasions, the record showed that Russia's behaviour was unaffected by the prospect of deterrence or non-deterrence. The issue was not to craft policy based on Russia's perceived intentions but with a view to compelling Russia to accede to the international rule of law and reverse its actions. It was necessary for the alliance to demonstrate that there were costs associated with waging war. It was also necessary to respond simply because of what Russian aggression represented. "The current situation demands – beyond sanctions, financial and technical assistance – even firmer and more robust measures," the UCC argued, "to prevent Russia from realizing its political, economic and military objectives vis-à-vis Ukraine, which would have grave consequences for European security and international stability."[33] With the NATO summit to convene on 4 September 2014, the UCC national executive stated, "Canada and its allies must decide."

At issue were the security guarantees, particularly in the form of the Budapest Memorandum, which had been extended to Ukraine in exchange for relinquishing its share of the Soviet nuclear arsenal. The UCC queried: "If there is not a heavy price for Russia to pay for its invasion of Ukraine, then what do we say to China in the South China Sea? What do we say to Iran as it seeks to pursue nuclear weapons? What do we say to North Korea and the Korean peninsula?"[34] The UCC drew on the notion that the Ukrainian crisis was symptomatic of a wider geopolitical issue. The norms underpinning the international order were under attack and trust was eroding. Would the coalition come together and force rogue states to abide by standards, or stand idly by?

Bob Onyschuk, founding director of the Canada-Ukraine Chamber of Commerce, invoking the historical antecedents of the Munich Agreement and the Cuban Missile Crisis, asked whether the Western alliance would resist those who breached treaties and custom. "Will Barack Obama, David Cameron and the rest of the West call Vladimir Putin to task over this, as President John F. Kennedy did with Nikita Khrushchev? Or will they play the role of Neville Chamberlin, and call it 'peace for our time'?"[35] The historical references were not a coincidence. International peace and security were at stake, and a failure to defend the existing order would have far-reaching consequences. Community leaders made plain that the government needed to recognize both the seriousness of the moment and the importance of assisting Ukraine: "Vladimir Putin has turned Russia into [a] rogue and state sponsor of terror. Ukrainians cannot stop him without real international support."[36]

While Canada's pro-Ukraine agenda was in keeping with its commitment to the international order, this support was determined by the US and the constraints on its leadership. To the degree that Canada's behaviour was an expression of its middle-power status – highlighting its role as a "price taker" rather than "price maker" – Canada would reciprocate in a manner that was in keeping with this status.[37] Anything else would have been disadvantageous in the long run and certainly done nothing to help Canada's credibility where it mattered most – Washington.[38] This, however, did not mean that Canada was without strategic interests or objectives. Rather, Canada seized every opportunity to signal its support for the international order in the clearest possible manner, even when US cautiousness was in evidence. To this end, certain specifically crafted bilateral initiatives – not only rhetoric – would play an important role in making Canada's position evident and eliminating any possible ambiguity regarding the need to stand with Ukraine.

CONCLUSION

Neoclassical realism generally assigns primacy to system-level variables as a way to understand state behaviour and leadership decisions. This case is no exception. Given the gravity of the Ukrainian crisis, the Harper government's policy can primarily be explained in terms of Canada's commitment to maintaining and supporting the international order. Specifically, the government's Ukraine policy was formulated in response to imperatives born of a system under attack, but also with US leadership in mind. In this instance, international dynamics proved decisive in shaping Canada's strategic approach, as did its middle-power status, its capabilities, and its role in the coalition.

The key issue, of course, was Russia's challenge to the existing order. Peace depended on security and stability. As such, the threat to peace posed by Russia had to be addressed. But this threat was also accompanied by a set of different challenges. The possibility of widening the conflict was real. Additionally, there was the uncertainty associated with the US, which had not only grown weary of carrying out its traditional role after years of war but also exhibited uncharacteristic caution in its outlook and behaviour as system leader. How then was Canada to respond? As in the past, Canada would seek to shore up system stability by participating in the coalition effort. It would also look to elevate the level of opposition to Russia. The Canadian response, in this regard, was deliberate and considered, one that spoke to circumstances.

The government resorted, initially, to using strident language to communicate its expectations and objectives, responding to key imperatives such as upholding the rules-based order and maintaining Canada's place and role as a coalition partner. Reflecting the risks if the order were to collapse, the vociferous nature of the rhetoric was also an attempt on Canada's part to persuade other coalition states that the threat was real. Russia's actions threatened everyone, and the best way to thwart its ambitions was to support Ukraine's sovereignty and territorial integrity. With this in mind, the Harper government was unequivocal

The Ukrainian Crisis, Canada, and World Order 43

and unambiguous in its critique, pushing back against the Russian narrative that Ukraine was either a manufactured project or a failed state while firmly laying responsibility for the conflict at the doorstep of Russia's leadership.

To the degree that the threat mounted, however, Canada would look to employ other specific measures – increasing support for both the economy and reforms in Ukraine – in order to institutionally strengthen the Ukrainian state in its fight with Russia. It was an intensive bilateral effort on Canada's part, underscoring the importance of Ukraine as a strategic priority. But this effort was also aimed at addressing a wider strategic objective. Failing to defend the international order, as constructed, or to ignore the principles at stake would have been tantamount to abandoning it while opening the door to instability. Systemic defence was primary and Ukraine's role in that defence was pivotal, accounting for the Harper government's strategic focus on Ukraine and the augmented bilateral assistance effort.

Yet, this strategic perspective was coupled with the need to tread carefully. It was paramount that the situation not spiral out of control. Highlighting the difficulty of subscribing to principle within a strategic environment, the Harper government would deflect appeals by the Ukrainian-Canadian community to intervene directly and to do more. A sign of restraint, it had to be offset, however, by other indicators that would demonstrate the sincerity of Canadian intentions and communicate the urgency of the moment. The deployment of trainers in Ukraine and military assets in Eastern Europe were just such markers. The Ukrainian crisis, in effect, served as a test of Canada's commitment to the international order, defending it against challengers while demonstrating its role as a dependable partner by advancing the interests of the coalition without jeopardizing it. The Harper government sought to do this responsibly, by engaging Ukraine bilaterally with global security and stability in mind.

There was, however, one additional challenge that faced the Harper government: how to ensure that public opinion was behind the government's policy? It was crucial that Canadians understand why Ukraine was a strategic priority. As a strategic concern linked to wider, notional ideas about global security, this was hard to explain. Moreover, the measures being undertaken were potentially risky, with the possibility of blowback, and Ukraine was far away. Why was it in Canada's national interest to assist this country? The Harper government, in effect, was confronted with the issue of how to persuade Canadians, in a tangible and meaningful way, that the threat was both real and of consequence.

3

The Crisis and Canadian Interests: Canada's Support for Ukraine

Neoclassical realism is concerned in part with how domestic factors condition state responses to changing systemic circumstances. Within this framework, variables such as political culture, partisan political interests, civil society actors, and economic considerations significantly shape the foreign policy process. Representing incentives and constraints, these can either reinforce or restrict a state's behaviour, thereby affecting how the national interest is pursued or whether it is pursued at all.[1] Not surprisingly, accounting for these considerations allows for a more robust foreign policy analysis. It clarifies, for example, why certain foreign policy decisions and initiatives are undertaken, and why comparably ranked states sometimes pursue different responses under similar conditions. It also helps to explain the nation's interest with respect to the existing international order and any threats it may face.

The latter is particularly germane. Ideas and values are important foreign policy considerations which states pursue. The willingness to defend the rules-based order, for example, highlights the proposition that normative policy goals matter. But why is this the case, especially in relation to other interests, and what is the process that would elevate political culture to the status of a national interest? Moreover, how precisely does this affect a country's foreign policy? And how do values, practically speaking, translate into foreign policy initiatives, particularly under threatening circumstances?

The Harper government's response to the Ukrainian crisis mirrored its assessment of Canada's foreign policy interests in relation to Russia's challenge to the international order. The aim of the Harper government, however, was to impress upon Canadians that the threat was not distant and abstract, but immediate and real, by emphasizing the connection between the principles underpinning the liberal order and the political values that Canadians cherished. To protect the international order was to defend Canadian values, and the best way to safeguard these, as an interest, was to work alongside coalition partners against those who would overturn the order. But what effect did this melding of interests and values have on Canada's foreign policy direction? Did it constitute a policy shift? Furthermore, what did this fusion entail and how was it received?

During Stephen Harper's tenure as prime minister, Canadian interests would play an important, determinative role in shaping Canada's response to the Ukrainian crisis. They would do so, however, in a very specific way, drawing attention to the link that existed between international order and those values that aligned with Canada's political culture. In this way, particular meaning was imparted both to Russia's challenge and the Canadian response, lending weight and significance to each while assisting the Harper government in mobilizing support for those efforts that aimed to preserve and defend the existing order. This would inevitably draw the government closer to the Ukrainian-Canadian community, which, primed to assist Ukraine, also spoke of Canadian values. But, practically speaking, what did an alignment between values and interests mean? And what would best reflect Canada's interests and serve as appropriate and meaningful undertakings in the context of the crisis? Foreign policy initiatives and the forms they assume reveal much about a state's interests. The nature of Canada's foreign policy behaviour in support of Ukraine would be no exception.

SITUATING CANADA'S FOREIGN POLICY INTERESTS

Under Stephen Harper, Canada's response to the crisis in Ukraine proved to be unusual in that it did not draw on those international institutions, like the UN, that were traditionally associated with Canadian foreign policy.[2] Nor did it follow the pattern of moderation that characterized Canada's foreign policy past. This was evident in the boldness of the government's rhetoric and some of its actions, both of which more closely resembled those of a major power. These placed Canada at the forefront of the coalition's response to the crisis, leaving some observers struggling for an explanation. Indeed, the Harper government's new-look foreign policy did not signal a sudden gain in influence. So how might the forcefulness of its rhetoric and actions be understood and explained?

Foreign policy is shaped by factors at the global level; balances of power, for example, influence the behaviour of states. Yet, arguably, foreign policy also involves the pursuit or defence of interests based on a crude calculation of benefits, costs, and needs. Therefore, were interests at work here that might explain Canada's actions? How did these relate to priorities established by global circumstances, if at all? The answer to these questions may very well begin with neoclassical realism's acknowledgment that foreign policy makers, operating domestically and internationally, seek to balance or manage opportunities and constraints at both levels.[3] An important insight, it reminds us that developments at multiple levels intersect in a way that is consequential in giving direction and shape to a state's foreign policy.

For example, even though international considerations may frame a state's behaviour, the specific political character of a state can be problematic, especially if it harbours ambitions and possesses the requisite capabilities to pursue them.[4] In the context of a liberal order, an illiberal state possessing significant power resources is often perceived to be a threat. Leaders that ignore such threats do so at their peril. A liberal state, consequently, seeks to resist the actions of states that oppose the liberal order and, frequently, ally with states of similar character. Thus, the political character of states is said to play a role in shaping policy direction and leadership perspectives. Still, this does not explain the spirited character of Canada's response during the Ukrainian crisis. To be sure, from the perspective of stability and the liberal state, the defence of the Western rules-based order constituted an interest while an illiberal state in possession of significant power, such as Russia, represented a genuine threat. But did not Canada and its allies stand in defence of the liberal order throughout the Cold War? Did not the USSR represent at least as much of a risk at that time? So, why was Canada responding now in such a vigorous manner?

Since 1945, the defence of the liberal order was considered a strategic priority for all member states of the Western coalition.[5] After the collapse of the Soviet Union, it was a foregone conclusion that international relations would conform to the liberal ethos. Not surprisingly, however, when the existing order came under attack in 2014, the Harper government consciously framed its defence (and, correspondingly, its support for Ukraine) as a national interest. It did so because of what was at stake. The norms and principles sustaining a stable and secure order were at risk. However, if abstract international principles such as freedom and sovereign right were to be accepted as national interests, then these had to resonate with Canadians. To realize this, the government would emphasize alignment between the two while advancing the argument that the defence of international principles was tantamount to protecting the values associated with Canada's political heritage and identity. Significantly, it was an argument made in the context of a cultural shift occurring in Canada and the partisan struggle for the country's political future, including its foreign policy.

A feature of the Harper government's foreign policy was its apparent departure from past practice.[6] Internationalism, with its focus on multilateral diplomacy, had long been a cornerstone of Canadian foreign policy. First laid down by Liberal Prime Minister Lester Pearson, every Canadian leader since had adhered to it. Consequently, the public's perception that Pearson's foreign policy legacy was the most authentically Canadian ensured the Liberal Party's continuing lock on Canada's foreign policy tradition. For political reasons, it was important that the Harper government sever this link. It did so by emphasizing what were considered to be Canadian values and beliefs. Depicted as classical liberal in nature (with a focus on individual rights and freedoms),

The Crisis and Canadian Interests 49

these values resonated with the ideological tenets that informed the conservative, populist Reform movement, which had challenged (among other things) the reigning foreign policy paradigm's multilateral focus and affinity for global institutions.[7] Canada's new-look foreign policy, in effect, would draw on this interpretation of Canadian values to recalibrate the country's foreign policy principles and priorities, guiding its interests at home and abroad.

Both Liberals and traditional Tories had long held that it was in Canada's interest to defend the existing order because of the peace and stability it provided. Historically, peacekeeping under the aegis of the UN, as well as development aid and assistance, constituted important strategic goals in Canada's commitment to peace and security. The insurgent Reform movement, however, viewed the "human-rights-blind foreign policy" pursued by Canada throughout most of the post-1945 period as an inadequate reflection of Canadian ideals and interests. This position was principally grounded in the Reform Party's ideological commitment to a freedom and individual rights agenda. In Western Canada, where egalitarian conceptions of civil liberties ran deep, the Reform Party's radical re-conception of rights helped it gain grassroots support and, thus, political traction.[8] Stephen Harper would bring this perspective into government and draw upon it to frame Canada's approach to the world in the expectation that these ideals, expressed as foreign policy interests, would enhance the country's global stature and influence.[9]

With its emphasis on rights and freedoms, the Harper government's radical reinterpretation of liberalism, became a distinguishing feature of Canada's foreign policy. But so, too, was its take on the world as a place full of risk and peril.[10] Realist in outlook, this perspective informed the government's political take on Russia's behaviour under Vladimir Putin. Stephen Harper would assert in 2015 that Russia was "trying deliberately to be a strategic rival, to deliberately counter the good things we're trying to achieve in the world for no other reason than to just counter them."[11] Intended to serve as an indictment, it underlined Russia's intemperate behaviour while making it out to be an unavoidable adversary. But this assessment also keyed in on the idea that Canada was part of a larger strategic coalition and that the danger Russia posed, although aimed principally at the US, was ubiquitous; thus, Harper's general assertion that "threats to the United States are threats to Canada."[12] The importance of maintaining a close working relationship with the US could not have been clearer and explained the government's preference for US-dominated institutions, such as NATO, over more inclusive, multilateral global institutions.

Understandably, the Harper government would not lose sight of working within the boundaries of a security alliance as a foreign policy interest. Nor, however, would it lose sight of the deeper meaning and reason why this was case. The alliance was bound by a commitment to Western liberal ideas and ideals that not only underpinned the international order but also informed Canada's political culture. Therefore, to defend the governing order, according to the prime minister and his associates, was to defend core values – classical liberal in nature – that historically defined what it meant to be Canadian: "We use our might sparingly; but when we do so we do so with full conviction, gathering our forces as men and women who believe that the freedoms we enjoy cannot be taken away from us. This clarity focuses our might in terrible times. And wherever and whenever we unleash that might, we raise our grateful voices and our prayers to honour those who have stood in harm's way for us."[13]

It was a perspective that simultaneously tied the fate of the system not only to strategic concerns, but to ethical and identity concerns as well. Moreover, how these statements were interpreted strengthened Canada's resolve to fully support the US in the latter's objective of propagating freedom and democracy everywhere as means of stabilizing the existing order.[14] This proved pivotal in view of Russia's challenge.

Since the end of the Cold War, Canadian foreign policy discourse had little to say about the prospects of declining order or Canada's interest in system defence. The stability of the rules-based order was assumed a priori by past Canadian governments, with concern centred mainly on how it could be improved. This bias was expressed throughout the post–Cold War period, a time when destabilizing interstate conflicts were considered highly unlikely. Indeed, the changes in international conditions that began with the end of the Cold War meant that non-conventional security threats, such as international terrorism, would soon dominate Canadian security discourse. Yet, only powerful states possessed the ability to challenge and overturn the existing rules of the system – and certainly in a way that non-conventional threats could not. Within the international system, therefore, states continued to pose a singular risk to international security.

Indeed, when the Russia-Ukraine conflict erupted, the stability of the liberal order could no longer be taken for granted. For the first time in the post–Cold War era, Canadian foreign policy makers had to work under the assumption that the system and its guiding principles were vulnerable. Supporting the governing order, which had been a relatively passive undertaking in the post–Cold War period, became once again a political and strategic necessity. More importantly, the presence of a clear threat prompted the Harper government to begin reorienting Canada's foreign policy toward a Cold War–style system defence.

Like its predecessors, the Harper government maintained a degree of confidence in the stability of the rules-based order prior to the Ukrainian crisis. However, unlike his predecessors, Stephen Harper sensed that this order could be easily undone. Having spent much of his tenure as prime minister preoccupied with various threats to national security, the Ukrainian crisis of 2014 simply reinforced his pessimistic outlook while further undermining his confidence in the stability of the existing order.[15] It was at this juncture that the Harper government emerged as a staunch supporter of Ukraine and a harsh critic of Russia's aggression, fortified by the belief that values represented a vital national interest, which Canada was duty-bound to defend within the context of a system under attack.

Forged in the fire of the First World War, Prime Minister Harper considered Canada a "fighting country" with a strong and abiding interest in promoting and defending Canadian values as part of the liberal order.[16] Although historian Charlotte Gray observed that the use of this description would have been "unthinkable" under previous governments, it was a profound expression of the Harper government's unique sense of the country's history, identity, and destiny, distinguishing him from the leaders who came before him.[17] But it was also the case that he was forced to contend with a very different set of circumstances than those faced by his predecessors. Indeed, the Ukrainian crisis prompted a strategic response that was framed by the need to defend the rules-based order and which resonated with values deeply embedded in Canada's national psyche and history. The intersection of these factors would help define the Harper government's foreign policy response to the Ukrainian crisis. Nevertheless, a question remained: given the international challenge and Canada's interests, what would be the nature of Canada's support for Ukraine? Or, put differently: what initiatives in support of Ukraine would best reflect Canada's values as interests?[18]

THE NATURE OF THE HARPER GOVERNMENT'S ASSISTANCE TO UKRAINE

Russia's aggression against Ukraine brought Canada's interests into sharper focus. As the crisis deepened, Canada pursued these interests with more urgency than it had at any point since 1991. Of minimal importance to the Harper government because of the failed presidencies of Viktor Yushchenko and Viktor Yanukovych, the Canada-Ukraine relationship was now re-energized by the conflict.[19] What mattered, however, was not Ukraine per se, but rather what the aggression against Ukraine represented – a threat to the principles and norms that governed the liberal global order. It was the defence of these principles that would guide the Harper government's support for Ukraine and inform Canada's political and security response to the crisis.

The types of political/diplomatic action that the government would take were varied. Initially, symbolic gestures figured prominently. These were used to produce a response that explicitly and implicitly recognized the significance of the crisis while transmitting a statement about Canada's stance. The Ukrainian national flag,

The Crisis and Canadian Interests 53

for example, flew on Canada's Parliament Hill only days after the invasion.[20] Given the acute nature of the crisis, the gesture was conspicuous, unapologetically telegraphing to both domestic and foreign audiences that Canada stood in solidarity with Ukraine. To the new leadership in Kyiv, it signalled Canada's unwavering support. In Moscow, it communicated Ottawa's rejection of the argument that the crisis was a civil conflict. Ukrainian sovereignty was at issue, which the Harper government unequivocally endorsed. Ukraine would not be left to fend for itself.

Keenly aware of its hard-power limitations, however, the Harper government attempted diplomatically to leverage its soft power. At the outset of the crisis, the government quickly organized an exchange of high-profile state visits. On the heels of the Euromaidan and in an overt display of goodwill, the prime minister travelled directly to Ukraine – the first G7 leader to do so. There he would pay homage at a makeshift memorial to the fallen dead and meet with Ukrainian government officials to discuss ways in which Canada could immediately support Ukraine.[21] Meanwhile, Ukraine's newly elected president, Petro Poroshenko, was invited to come to Ottawa in September to deliver a speech in a joint address to Canada's parliament – a rare honour.[22] These and other diplomatic measures did not alter Russia's behaviour in any perceptible way. But this was not the intent. Rather, state-to-state engagement underscored the legitimacy being conferred on the new government by Canada.

Legitimacy was of paramount importance insofar as the Russian president, Vladimir Putin, was adamant that the new Ukrainian government was putschist in character and therefore illegitimate, having been brought about by armed revolt. Political recognition, consequently, was a necessary first step toward countering this narrative. Prime Minister Harper's presence at the June 7 installation of Poroshenko as Ukraine's president – one of a handful of world leaders at the ceremony – was part of this endeavour. Congratulatory statements following Ukraine's October 2014 parliamentary elections served this purpose as well. All of these measures signalled that Ukraine had a recognized government, thus publicly undercutting Putin's claim that there was "nobody to talk to" in Kyiv, while delegitimizing the Russian pretext for intervening in Ukraine.[23] It was not enough merely to offer an alternative to Russia's account of chaos in Ukraine; Canada sought to discredit and push back against Russia's dissembling narrative.[24]

No less important were the actions taken to convey Canada's disapproval with Russia's military foray into Ukraine. The Canadian ambassador to Moscow was withdrawn "for consultations" and Canada's preparations for the G8 Summit in Sochi were suspended (a body soon to be reduced in number with Russia's expulsion from that body).[25] The point of these and other initiatives was to make apparent to Russia that its behaviour was unacceptable. However, they were also meant to isolate Russia and accentuate its pariah status. Russia, alone, was responsible for its growing predicament. Only by ending its aggression and observing the touchstones of international relations – the sovereignty and independence of states – could Russia hope to recover its reputation as a respected global player. If it chose to ignore these and other warnings, then it could expect to be treated as an errant and scorned member of the international community. It could also expect for Canada to confront and treat Russia as an adversary, a position that linked defence of the international order with Canada's foreign policy priorities.

Even more broadly, the government sought to locate these priorities within the wider public arena by framing its position with reference to what were described as Canadian values: justice, freedom, and equality, among others. By invoking Canada's values, the government would enhance its mobilizing efforts as well as strengthen and legitimate its foreign policy objectives: "Canada stands for what is right and good in the world," declared David Johnston, Canada's governor general, in a speech from the throne. "This is the true character of Canadians – honourable in our dealings, faithful to our commitments, loyal to our friends. Confident partners, courageous warriors, and compassionate neighbours."[26] In the context of rising international tensions and threats, Jason Kenney, the defence minister, noted the important role that ethical considerations now played in Canada's external policy, asserting that "Canada had now become more relevant" and adding that Canadians, when called upon, "would defend what was right and necessary."[27]

The prominence of political culture in the Harper government's foreign policy and the willingness to defend Canadian values was apparent in other statements by senior government officials, including an important policy speech delivered in the wake of the Euromaidan by John Baird, the foreign affairs minister. Baird was forthright in his claim that in order to achieve peace and security, Canadian foreign policy had to "actively bat for the side of what's right."[28] Baird argued further that by promoting responsible democratic governance and laying the foundations for economic prosperity, Canada could help Ukraine realize these objectives. Canada's support for Ukraine, therefore, had both normative and applied dimensions.[29] To prevent Ukraine from devolving into a state of disarray that could possibly pose a possible danger to global security, its governance and economic structures had to be strengthened. As a result, the values that guided Canada's political support for Ukraine translated into a series of projects intended to bolster the latter's reputation as a state committed to the rule of law and an open economy.

Specifically, the Harper government took several practical yet principled steps to stabilize the economic situation in Ukraine. To this end, Canada reaffirmed Ukraine's status as a country of focus by listing it as a priority under the Global Markets and Action Plan. As part of this strategy, Canada pledged approximately $578 million in economic assistance, which included two separate $200 million low-interest loans.[30] The government further adopted measures to expand bilateral trade ties, conducting a number of quickly organized trade missions over the course of 2014–15, while declaring that negotiations toward an all-important bilateral free-trade agreement would resume.[31] Additionally, the government funded the work of Ukraine's Economic Advisory Council and announced it would collaborate with the Federation of Canadian Municipalities to support the long-term Partnership for Local Economic Development and Democratic

Governance project in Ukraine. Bolstered by the events on the Euromadian, this unique initiative would add to Canada's longstanding support for the liberal domestic reforms process in Ukraine, ensuring transparent and efficient decision making by local government. Empowering civil society, the "Revolution of Dignity" also had quickly given rise to local actors to whom Canada could now deliver specialized forms of aid and assistance. Not only did working with these groups strengthen Ukrainian civil society, it increased Canada's confidence in supporting several new electoral, legislative, judicial, and policing reform projects, including allocating $8 million for the Strengthening Multi-Party Democracy project.[32]

This effort, however, was not entirely altruistic. It reflected a conscious effort to ensure that Canadian interests were being addressed. In this regard, core values aligned with Canadian strategic objectives – promoting democracy and economic freedom. Yet, the political meaning and intent behind these initiatives did nothing to address the main issue: how to deter Russia. While the Harper government recognized that expanding economic, social, and political assistance to Ukraine was in Canada's interest, it understood that the success of these efforts would ultimately depend on the coalition's ability to dissuade Russia from further aggression. Deterrent measures were needed. Given the stakes involved, Canada would take an avid interest in supporting the US-led sanctions regime that was introduced to counteract Russian behaviour and even undo its effects.

Responding to Russia's aggression and non-compliance, sanctions were instituted. Initially targeting individuals directly tied to Russian belligerence, these were soon extended to broader sectors of the Russian economy, most notably Russia's banking system and its quasi-state-controlled oil-and-gas industry.[33] The effectiveness of the campaign, however, depended on cooperation. In this regard, Canada participated actively in the international effort, imposing the first set of sanctions against Russia on 18 March 2014 under the Special Economic Measures Act. The Harper government at times also took a strong lead, amending regulations twelve times to include even more individuals and commercial entities. This willingness to assume an assertive approach made plain the government's awareness of Canada's pivotal role in the shared defence of the system. More fundamentally, from a values perspective it underscored the Harper government's commitment to upholding the sovereignty of nations and a rules-bound order. As a result, the sanctions campaign was prioritized as a Canadian foreign policy interest.

Casting the sanctions regime in this role, however, had economic implications, redounding as it did on Canadian trade. There was also the question of optics. From the perspective of a business-friendly Conservative government, economic sanctions were anathema. Still, as Prime Minister Harper explained, the Canadian interest was more than the aggregate interest of Canadian businesses: "We don't like seeing any disruption to investment or markets or trade, but looking at it from the point of view of the greater national interest, an occupation of one country by another has serious long-term implications."[34] Explaining his government's actions, Harper declared that Canada's support was deemed necessary because Russia's flagrant disregard of the rules-based order jeopardized and undercut the political conditions that international trade and commerce required to thrive. Trade was not simply transactional; it was bound by rules and norms, and these needed to be observed and respected. Critics of the government, however, would point to Canada's limited trade with Russia, noting that the risks to Canada were minimal, thereby casting doubt on the sincerity and seriousness of the government's actions. Yet, the criticism unfairly ignored the intent and rationale behind the sanctions – they could only work if everyone participated and cooperated.

Canada signalled its commitment to defend the existing order by strengthening the Ukrainian state and imposing a sanctions regime. A goal that had been merely implicit in Canada's earlier foreign policy was now made explicit. Canada's strategic interests, therefore, were brought to the forefront of the Canada-Ukraine relationship. Moreover, by working with its coalition partners politically, diplomatically, and economically, Canada was doing everything possible to counteract Russia's behaviour. Nevertheless, the threat remained. Russian aggression continued unabated.

There was no question that with Russia's continuing belligerence, Ukraine faced serious challenges to its security. The question for Canada was what else could it do? The war threatened to expand as a result of Russia's extensive and growing involvement. Meanwhile, the routine violence in the conflict zones exacted a daily toll on innocent lives. Ukraine both needed and appealed for kinetic military equipment, including deadly Javelin anti-tank missiles and launchers. By altering the balance of power on the ground, however, lethal military assistance could have triggered a reaction from Russia, possibly escalating the conflict even further. There was also the requirement to work within the parameters of an alliance framework. The US, which exhibited caution as coalition leader, thus far had been reluctant to provide the weapons requested, even for defensive purposes. Consequently, for Canada, careful consideration had to be given as to what was needed, what was possible, and what might best help under the circumstances.

Set to assist but constrained by its alliance requirements, Canada would look to augment Ukraine's security through alternative means. In August 2014, Canada began delivering non-lethal, but nonetheless indispensable, military supplies in large quantities.[35] This materiel included thermal and night-vision goggles, ballistic vests and eyewear, tactical first-aid kits, communications devices, ordnance disposal equipment, cold-weather field gear, and a mobile field hospital. Further, Canada took the unusual step of providing Ukraine with access (albeit limited) to geospatial intelligence and continued to deliver supplies on a regular basis. Meanwhile, intending to warn Russia and deter it from further encroachments elsewhere in Eastern Europe, Canada contributed air and naval assets to NATO's Operation Reassurance. At the 2014 NATO summit in Wales, Prime Minister Harper touted Canada's efforts as a "leading contributor" to NATO's mission in Eastern Europe.[36] And this was before the April 2015 deployment of 200 Canadian

Armed Forces trainers to Ukraine as part of Canada's Operation Unifier. Contrasting with the UK and US contingents of 75 and 800 instructors respectively, the training mission would become the most salient aspect of Canada's security assistance to Ukraine.

Canada's support for Operation Unifier and Operation Reassurance placed it at the centre of NATO's efforts to enhance the coalition's defensive security posture against Russia. Although Canada gained vital intelligence about the effectiveness of combat tactics by working with battle-hardened Ukrainian troops, there was no denying the resoluteness of its commitment to and support for the coalition effort and Ukraine in particular. Indeed, providing military training assistance instead of preserving satisfactory relations with Russia demonstrated the extent to which Ukraine was seen not only as a Canadian security priority but also an ally. However, by defending Ukrainian democracy, the centrality of Canadian values in Canada's mission in Ukraine was also made clear.

Nowhere was this more evident than in Canada's commitment to peace-building measures, considered vital to safeguarding Ukraine's sovereignty and even facilitating an end to the conflict. On this point, the Harper government backed the European-brokered Minsk I (5 September 2014) and Minsk II (15 February 2015) ceasefire protocols while supporting the OSCE-led monitoring initiative beginning in March 2014.[37] Conducted under the aegis of the OSCE's Parliamentary Assembly and Office for Democratic Institutions and Human Rights, the initial task of the OSCE monitors was to gather information on the security and human rights situation in the conflict zones, report this information in a transparent and impartial fashion, and, in keeping with conflict resolution measures, facilitate a dialogue between the belligerents with the aim of de-escalating the conflict. Contributing twenty-five ground personnel and some $2.7 million to assist the mission, the Harper government signalled its intention to uphold human rights in the conflict zone.[38] It was an important initiative because the violation of human rights drew attention to the issue of international norms and the impact of war. But by assisting, the Harper government also sought to strengthen the monitoring regime with the hope of ending the violence, underscoring its values-based approach to the crisis.

Not surprisingly, the didactic character of Canada's foreign policy response – "batting for the right side of history" – resulted in criticism. Several pundits noted that Russia's actions were simply part of the normal functioning of a competitive international system. It was not unusual that states would pursue their political interests; therefore, they argued, Canadian foreign policy was best served by recognizing this reality.[39] A deeply cynical argument, it presumed that interests were tied to power considerations and that this alone was the sum and substance of foreign policy.

But more importantly, other critics pointed to the electoral influence of the diaspora on Canadian foreign policy, chiding the government for its partisanship. International relations specialists David Carment and Joseph Landry argued that "the government's hard line stance against Russia's involvement in the Ukrainian crisis appears to be driven by domestic politics and not by any larger geostrategic or moral imperatives," and that this was but part of a wider pattern of "diaspora pandering [that] converged with the government's ideological orientation, creating and reinforcing a nested policy agenda that appealed to a narrow political base at home while serving no core Canadian interests abroad, or, worse, generating hostility with homeland governments."[40] The Russian foreign minister, Sergei Lavrov, advanced a similar charge, denouncing the Harper government for "blindly following the demands of rabid representatives of the Ukrainian diaspora in Canada, simply ignoring their own national interests."[41]

The description of ethnic pandering, of course, speaks to stereotype, which either mischaracterizes the nature of the relationship or fails to understand it altogether. With a long history of settlement in Canada and integrated within the social and political fabric of the country, Ukrainian Canadians are politically pluralist in their beliefs and political allegiances. This suggests that political solicitation based on a quid pro quo would have been pointless if not meaningless. More to the point, however, the nature of the relationship between the government and the community was reciprocal in that both parties shared a common understanding of the problem: it was Russia's violation of international norms and treaty obligations that had led to war and brought about suffering among the innocents. This conclusion, although arrived at separately, was a shared one because both parties were inclined to view the crisis through the same values-based lens.

For Paul Grod, president of the Ukrainian Canadian Congress, this values-based perspective began for Ukrainian Canadians with the story of their immigrant journey.[42] Ukrainian immigrants contributed to building the country with their arrival in Canada, creating in the process a mutual history based on some simple but widely held truths – the importance of personal dignity, freedom, and peace. Aspiring to the same goals and driven by the same expectations, "we have found that Ukraine and Ukrainians are fundamentally like Canadians" and that "Canadian values were Ukrainian values."[43] In giving testament to those shared values, however, Grod also observed that without Canadian assistance, Ukraine's path forward would be difficult. Nevertheless, within the context of the crisis he remained hopeful, if only because the sentiment around such shared values made for both a common understanding of Canada's foreign policy principles and priorities, and a heightened appreciation of the challenges ahead. It also necessarily made for cooperation between the government and the community.[44]

This focus on values naturally tailored the type of assistance that the Ukrainian-Canadian community would provide to Ukraine in its moment of need. Specifically, material support assumed the form of humanitarian and medical assistance, conducted under the UCC's Ukraine Appeal campaign. Maximizing the effectiveness of Canadian aid and assistance efforts, the initiative sought to coordinate the activities of donors, volunteers, and even provincial governments seeking to assist the victims of Russia's war in Ukraine – all of which complemented Ottawa's humanitarian contributions.[45] Whether it was setting up rehabilitation programs, delivering donated ambulances, or offering logistical support to tens of thousands in need among the internally displaced, the community delivered on an impressive scale. So, too, did its provisioning of medical supplies for frontline troops – haemostatic dressings, shears, surgical sutures, medications, blankets. The diaspora looked to make a meaningful difference. As one recipient commented regarding the value of such assistance: "At least now we know that someone cares about us."[46]

The threat of Russian escalation, of course, was never far from the minds of Ukrainian Canadians, and the UCC urged the Harper government to support Ukraine with much-needed armaments.[47] Military assistance, however, was a state-to-state matter. The primary focus, therefore, would continue to be on humanitarian aid, which underscored the need to work within established parameters while deflecting possible criticism that ordinary Canadians were directly involved and adding to the conflict. Ukrainian Canadians, in effect, were helping in ways that made sense as members of Canadian civil society and in accordance with the laws and values upheld by Canadian society more widely. Moreover, the aid provided was in keeping with Canadian priorities and interests. This, it was said, was what Canadians did and were expected to do. But perhaps most importantly, the assistance would help alleviate the suffering. As Dr. Oleh Antonyshyn, the lead surgeon in the Canada-Ukraine Surgery Mission program, remarked following a mercy mission to Ukraine that resulted in fifty-eight procedures: "These surgeries were never going to happen, if we didn't do them."[48]

The Ukrainian crisis came as an inflection point. Would Ukraine continue down the path of becoming a functioning democracy that prized political transparency and an open society, or would it be pulled back into Russia's orbit? Committed as they were to democracy, rule of law, and freedoms, Canadians, according to the polls, were inclined to side with Ukraine as the country struggled to chart a democratic course.[49] In this sense, it was natural that the Harper government would champion the right of Ukrainians to choose freely. From the perspective of the government, and especially of Prime Minister Harper, to stand with Ukraine was to stand for Canadian values and, in the process – as he and his cabinet colleagues were wont to declare – to

The Crisis and Canadian Interests 63

be on "the right side of history." This message – which echoed through the government's various assistance initiatives – complemented the efforts of the Ukrainian-Canadian diaspora, which was equally invested in helping Ukraine. It was also a message that resonated with the majority of Canadians, who widely agreed that the fight was in keeping with Canada's values and, therefore, interests.

CONCLUSION

Threatening international stability, Russia's aggression toward Ukraine triggered a coalition response. From Canada's point of view, support for democratic ideas and principles (including rule of law) aligned with the need to maintain the stability of a rules-based order, thus easing the way for the Harper government to support Ukraine. Public opinion was also firmly behind this decision. In part, this was due to the government advancing a narrative around the crisis that resonated with Canadians. Emphasizing the connection between national interest and political culture, this foreign policy orientation served as a powerful platform through which the Harper government could rally support. That it also afforded the government an opportunity to increase its credibility and thereby neutralize the Liberal Party's historical lock on Canada's foreign policy tradition was a bonus.

The Harper government's ability to mobilize public support for its international agenda was of importance to its political fortunes – but it was also important from the point of view of the scope and success of its policies. Indeed, if the government felt constrained by public opinion, it would have been disinclined to help with the type and robustness of action that circumstances called for. In 2014–15, the imperatives associated with a system in crisis demanded such a response, and with public opinion firmly in favour of the government's position, it was well situated to pursue an energetic reply without being hemmed in. Had Canadians taken an opposite view of the crisis, the resulting political constraints would have had an impact on the government's decision. This might not have completely altered the government's policy choice – after all, Canada was part of a broader coalition – but it may have tempered the forcefulness of its response.

If the Harper government's engagement was seen as defending values in a manner that was consistent with the national interest, how then are we to explain the apparently waning enthusiasm of the subsequent Liberal government? Is the Trudeau government not equally committed to a values-based foreign policy and just as interested in defending the existing international order? A mechanistic explanation that centres on the role of the international political structure and on foreign policy interests understates the significance of leadership in conditioning the shape and direction of Canada's response to the crisis. According to neoclassical realism, agency matters. Therefore, in order to fully understand Canada's Ukraine policy, Stephen Harper's role as a key foreign policy maker must also be taken into consideration. His worldview and understanding of politics would not only inform his threat assessments and policy preferences but also influence Canada's response, lending it colour and effect.

4

The Leadership of Stephen Harper: Agency, Worldview, and the Ukrainian Crisis

A basic assumption of neoclassical realist theory is that leaders have influence over the direction of a state's foreign policy.[1] This assumption is based on the view that foreign policy is informed by perceptions of state interest, which are often a reflection of certain objectives that political leaders champion based on their own set of ideas and beliefs. These mental landscapes not only form leaders' perspectives regarding opportunities and challenges, but their policy preferences as well. Recognizing the influential role that a leader's worldview plays assists us in understanding why similarly positioned states respond to challenges and opportunities in different and sometimes unexpected ways. It also helps account for the changing nature of foreign policy priorities from one government to another. But what, precisely, is the nature of the process through which aspects of leadership shape the pursuit of state interests? Do leaders exercise genuine autonomy in this process? Are the views expressed and actions taken simply a reflection of international considerations?

Canada's response to the Ukrainian crisis was unusually direct and robust. From the outset, Prime Minister Stephen Harper opposed Russia's aggression against Ukraine and gave voice to the importance of defending international norms and the rule of law. This emphasis on values would shape Canadian foreign policy in a particular way. Yet, it did not end there. The Harper government's approach and ethic, aligned with what was considered Canada's wider strategic interest of preserving the status quo under US leadership, was complicated by America's retrenchment during this period. The political leadership concluded, therefore, that Canada had a responsibility to increase its level of commitment. This became manifest in Harper's policy measures and his use of strident, didactic rhetoric, all of which were framed both by the prime minister's ideological defence of Canada's response and appeal to moral duty as a reply to the ambiguity of politics. Not surprisingly, when the role of agency is considered, Canadian foreign policy under Harper's watch assumed a distinctive quality.

But what precisely was the connection between political leadership, national interest, and international considerations? How and why did leadership attitudes develop in such a way that they would impact Canada's response to the crisis? What was the nature of this impact? And how were these perspectives received? Leadership perspectives would play a pivotal role. These are shaped, however, by a specific set of circumstances, which in this case included a period of domestic change that witnessed the emergence of a new conservative elite in Canada with definite and distinct ideas about the political and moral content of Canada's foreign policy. How this would affect leadership choices and the statements made would reveal itself in the context of the Ukrainian crisis. In the process, the foreign policy of the conservative Harper government would distinguish itself while resonating with a diaspora that also looked for leadership at this critical moment.

DEFENDING ORDER: STRATEGY AND WORLDVIEW

Stephen Harper's worldview incorporated a mixture of principles that shaped his perception of strategic imperatives. As an advocate of the ideas associated with classical liberalism, the prime minister demonstrated little patience or tolerance for any form of politics that infringed either on liberty or the conditions that would allow for its wider propagation.[2] This framework informed a belief and values system that would guide the prime minister's understanding of international politics and Canada's place in the world.[3] Indeed, Harper viewed global politics as a competition between ideologies, and, like Ronald Reagan and Margaret Thatcher before him, considered certain philosophies to be inherently dangerous. Any ideology that denied freedom, he maintained, had to be resisted, arguing "that the great geopolitical battles against modern tyrants are battles over values."[4] These and other ideas led some to describe Harper's worldview as "black-and-white," Manichaean, or neoconservative. Such hard-and-fast characterizations, however, have generally done little to further understanding of his foreign policy decisions.[5] Rather, Harper's worldview was inspired by a variety of intellectual sources, at the core of which lay classical liberal ideas and principles. Given their importance to the evolving global order, he fundamentally believed that these had to be safeguarded against the ambitions of those who would seek to reverse history's gains.[6]

Stephen Harper's worldview remained consistent over time. His perception of the international environment as precarious was reinforced by the massive systemic shocks that occurred over two decades: the collapse of the Soviet Union, the 9/11 terror attacks against the United States, and the 2008 global financial crisis. Russia's aggression against Ukraine in 2014 provided additional evidence of the international system's volatile nature. If the close of the Cold War signalled "the end of history," the string of crises that defined the first decades of the new millennium trumpeted its return.[7] Faced with this new and daunting reality, Prime Minister Harper would come to characterize the world as a perilous and threatening place.[8] This preoccupation reflected the significant interplay between his threat assessments, his policy preferences, and the strength of his convictions.

Doing little to temper his enthusiasm for the classical liberal ideas and principles which he believed needed to be defended and promoted, the shocks to the global political and economic systems reinforced Stephen Harper's realism. He was convinced that system stability primarily depended upon US willingness to shoulder the burden of global leadership. This willingness, however, had become increasingly dependent on the material and moral support of coalition states. Helping to offset the growing strains of leadership, Harper recognized this increased need in light of the mounting challenges. He warned, "Canadians have to be prepared to contribute more."[9] Thus, Stephen Harper, the consummate realist, would acknowledge that following the US was a first-order strategic imperative and coalition support a necessity.

Canada's pro-US vision of world order was hardly surprising given its historical relationship with America. However, accepting the US global agenda consisted of more than issuing declarations of support. It was also about reinforcing the sense among Canadians that there was an affinity between Canada and the beliefs and values at the heart of the liberal project. In a speech before the UN General Assembly in 2014, Prime Minister Harper declared that "Canadians believe freedom, prosperity and peace form a virtuous cycle."[10] This idea drove his conviction that for these to be achieved, the overarching goal of Canadian policy had to be to defend the liberal idea in places where it already existed – just as Canadians had done in the past – and to advance the idea further as circumstances permitted. To this end, the prime minister invoked historical images of Canada's military participation in the great struggles of the past while attending veterans' gatherings, Remembrance Day services across the country, and commemorative ceremonies at Vimy Ridge, Hong Kong, Normandy, and Arnhem, in the Netherlands. At each of these occasions, he spoke of the sacrifices that Canadians had made in the name of freedom. He also emphasized the historical role that the military played as an instrument of Canadian foreign policy.[11]

To be sure, Canada's past prime ministers and governments had been no less committed to supporting the liberal order throughout the many years of the Cold War. However, the Harper government differed by its decision to assimilate American strategic views and couch them in values that resonated with Canadians. When the Mulroney government helped to safeguard the stability of the international order during the collapse of the Soviet Union, it acted cautiously – for the most part simply mimicking US strategy.[12] In contrast, the Harper government went beyond mimicry and internalized both America's mission and the normative values associated with it. Indeed, the government's energetic response to the Ukrainian crisis reflected the extent to which new Canadian conservatives and Stephen Harper in particular came to accept the American mission as their own, marking an important political shift and ideological difference between Harper and his predecessors.

This assimilation of the US mission was the result of a long process of elite socialization that began with the appearance of the Reform Party in 1987. It occurred when Reform conservatives, emerging as a new political force in Canada, increasingly accepted and internalized the values and vision of the US as a global hegemon – a process that accelerated as a result of unexpected change in the international system.[13] Indeed, the way the Cold War ended enhanced the credibility of America's role in support of the liberal project, and reciprocally increased the confidence of Reform conservatives in the merits of following it. Mutually reinforcing, this process conditioned them to "internalize the norms and value orientations espoused by the hegemon and accept its normative claims about the nature of the international system."[14] Indeed, the degree of reciprocation following the end of the Cold War resulted in even a greater willingness to follow the US and accept its project for international peace and stability. All of this, however, would occur in the context of a cultural shift in Canada.

The rise of the populist Reform Party and the collapse of the USSR – separate but concurrent events – marked the beginning of a new discussion in Canada about its place in the world. Specifically, those who gravitated toward the Reform movement often harboured disdain for certain tendencies in Canada's foreign policy past. These individuals were especially skeptical of Canada's "human-rights-blind foreign policy," which they believed did not reflect the full range of values and beliefs held by Canadians.[15] Moreover, the insurgent Reformers viewed the traditional political establishment of Liberals and progressive Tories alike – the so-called "Laurentian consensus" – as being disinterested in promoting and defending the ideals that were considered central to Canadian identity.[16] The Reform critique was particularly appealing in Western Canada, where antipathy toward

Ottawa ran deep and the Laurentian dismissal of Canadian values as quaint anachronisms elicited resentment.

The irony was that many of these same ideals – freedom and individual rights, for example – were linked with the American historical experience.[17] Despite its paradoxical nature, this common and shared emphasis was not a coincidence. As a rising political class, Reform conservatives internalized the system leader's values, which meshed with their own ideological predilections. This was made possible because the process of socialization – which accelerated during this period of disorder – helped reshape the strategic and political preferences of influential Canadian conservatives. As elites became ideologically amenable to US objectives, they became more supportive of, if not acquiescent to, America's role.

This process of elite socialization helps to flesh out our understanding of the general shape and direction of Canadian foreign policy under Stephen Harper. In describing his government as "extremely pro-American," Prime Minister Harper made clear his identification with the US mission and its project for global security.[18] However, it also proved challenging, as American leadership under President Barack Obama increasingly displayed caution, a legacy of the wars in Afghanistan and Iraq. Both factors – Stephen Harper's pro-US orientation and America's reticent leadership – would have important implications in framing Canada's international engagement, guiding the prime minister's Ukraine policy during and immediately after the events on the Euromaidan. Stephen Harper's embrace of America's global agenda was unprecedentedly vigorous and unambiguous. However, he also wanted the US to go much further in supporting Ukraine.[19] Principles were at stake. The defence of Ukraine was a litmus test of the strength and resilience of the rule-based order. The response of the coalition states would provide a clear statement about how committed they were to its preservation.

The government's reaction to the crisis reflected the extent to which Stephen Harper (and the new Canadian conservative elites more generally) had internalized the American vision of world order. This trait in part distinguished him from the traditional

Laurentian elites, who regarded unchecked American power as a source of instability. From the prime minister's perspective, it was not the untrammelled power of the US that was at issue; rather, it was America's diminishing power and influence that threatened system stability.[20] The prime minister had identified this threat early on when, in 2012, he observed that "the ability of ... the United States to single-handedly shape outcomes and protect our interests has been diminishing."[21] Eschewing the unyielding commitment to multilateralism that had been embedded in the Laurentian consensus, the Harper government's response to the Ukrainian crisis was premised on both the pivotal role of the US and how Canada could assist it in preserving the status quo.[22] Canada's fulsome support for Ukraine and opposition to Russia, in effect, was meant to offset the mounting strains of leadership that had led to America's retrenchment.

The strength of Prime Minister Harper's support for the US's global agenda after the Euromaidan reflected the importance he attached to discouraging any further retreat. In 2003, Jean Chrétien, typifying the Laurentian attitude and approach at the time, appeared unfazed that his government's unwillingness to support the US-led war in Iraq might discourage American leadership. By 2014, however, traditional Laurentian elites were no longer managing Canada's foreign policy, and the new set of leaders in Ottawa were clearly less skeptical about the utility of American influence and strength in the context of the rising challenge. Moreover, unlike the Mulroney government, they were not interested in simply mimicking US strategy. Through the process of elite socialization, the new conservatives, led by Stephen Harper, had accepted America's mission as their own.

This changing of the guard precipitated a significant shift in thinking about the strategic direction of Canadian foreign policy. Unlike the Liberals, the Harper Conservatives were unwilling to jeopardize Canada's relationship with the US because they viewed close Canada-US relations as a first-order strategic imperative. The Harper government's posture toward the US, in this sense, was unlike that of its Liberal predecessors, whose policies tended to have a latent anti-American bias. And although Stephen Harper may have felt that the US response to Russia's conduct fell short under President Obama, it was better than no response.[23] The forcefulness of Canada's reaction, on the other hand, reflected the prime minister's firm belief that it was incumbent upon Canada to support America's global leadership, especially when it was weak or indecisive. This imperative was only strengthened by the danger and uncertainty of the historical moment that was at hand. With revisionist forces on the march, the coalition could not afford to send signals of disunity or weakness.

THE TENETS OF LEADERSHIP AND THE UKRAINIAN CRISIS

Stephen Harper was the most readily identifiable member of the new conservative elite that governed Canada from 2006 to 2015. Their rise coincided with multiple, overlapping crises that created a volatile and fragile political environment. During such periods, elites "seek alternatives to existing norms that have been discredited by events and in which new norms offer opportunities for political gains and coalitional realignment."[24] Thus, Canada's new conservatives not only acceded to America's normative ideals, they embraced and internalized them as their own. Most importantly, however, they exhibited none of the anti-American suspicion that helped sustain the Laurentian consensus.[25] This feature represents a key to understanding the shape and course of Canadian foreign policy under Stephen Harper and the contrast with what had preceded it. Following the Second World War, Canada supported the construction of a US-led global order, but latent anti-Americanism retarded the socialization process and prevented some Laurentian elites from fully internalizing the American vision. As a result, Canada's support for America's agenda appeared perfunctory, with various governments even withholding support on occasion.

All of this would change when Stephen Harper assumed office. The contrast with the past could not have been starker. In a meeting between Harper and Margaret Thatcher – a staunch supporter of America – the former British prime minister impressed upon him the importance of aligning closely with the US, especially in view of its foundational role in maintaining the rules-based order. With US global leadership under pressure and given his pro-American disposition, it was advice Harper had no trouble taking to heart.[26] No prime minister before or since had embraced the US and its vision of world order so openly, and no other prime minister had so clearly reshaped Canadian foreign policy to be more supportive of the US mission and its goals.[27] This orientation was especially evident in the Harper government's Ukraine policy.

Canada's willingness to follow was not tempered by Laurentian anti-Americanism. Rather, it was unequivocal and reflected Harper's strong pro-American stance. Instead of attempting to serve as a counterbalance to the US, the Harper government actively looked to support the US by embracing its ideological goals and strategic role in defending the international order from challengers who sought to revise it.[28] The full extent of the Harper government's embrace of this commitment became clear following Russia's invasion of Ukraine in 2014, which Stephen Harper referred to as "a wake-up call."[29] The prime minister further anticipated that Russia's actions would not only lead to its isolation, but that these would also amplify "the free world's unwavering fervour."[30] His remarks, far from being measured statements, mirrored political beliefs that had been formed by a particularly adversarial and uncompromising outlook.

Adam Chapnick would characterize this new brand of conservative foreign policy thinking, mainly associated with the prime minister, as "unCanadian" insofar as it did not follow the traditional tenets that had governed Canada's past international engagement.[31] From the point of view of the Harper Conservatives, however, Canada's new foreign policy would have been better described as "un-Laurentian." It was a vision that bore a striking resemblance to the position Harper had laid out earlier as the Reform Party's chief policy officer. "Canada's conduct in foreign as well as domestic affairs," Harper declared in 1988, "should be guided by the values and principles of Canadians as embodied in a system of dynamic and constructive change – political democracy and economic freedom. We should uphold and promote this legacy of human rights and dignity for all humanity."[32] Harper foreshadowed the direction Canadian foreign policy would take during his tenure as prime minister, and the broad outlines of his thinking remained consistent throughout his political career.

The consistency in his position was predicated on two points. First, Harper saw value in working to ensure that the existing rules-based order did not give way to the "law of the jungle."[33] His disposition toward this view was informed by an ethic that strengthened his political appreciation for "the benefits and benevolence of US hegemony."[34] Second, while Stephen Harper never identified himself as a neoconservative, he nonetheless shared with them the perspective that there was no viable alternative to a US-led order. As such, it would strengthen his resolve to support America in its bid to contain Russia's revisionist challenge.

This perspective was guided by the Canadian prime minister's strategic assessment of the state of the global system. But it also derived from his understanding of history. For Harper, the twentieth century provided ample evidence regarding the dangers associated with those attempts that sought to revise the international order by using force to achieve dubious goals. He pointed to Germany's annexation of the Sudetenland in 1938, which set in motion a chain of calamitous events that resulted in the Second World War. From Harper's perspective, Russia's invasion of Ukraine was akin to Nazi Germany's attack on Czechoslovakia, representing a strikingly similar and dangerously destabilizing revision of the European status quo.[35] The analogy, however overstated and jarring, was nevertheless meant to highlight the significant risk of allowing an aggressor state the freedom to seize territory and violate the sovereignty and independence of neighbouring states. From a historical perspective, and given Canada's interest in preserving the existing order, the government's strong opposition to Russian expansionism was seen as rational and reasonable. As Harper argued, Canada and its coalition partners' failure to confront Russia would only have emboldened Vladimir Putin, just as European appeasement had done with Germany in

The Leadership of Stephen Harper 75

the lead-up to the Second World War. "Our foreign policy," he noted, "obviously incorporates those kinds of lessons."[36]

This sense of history significantly informed Stephen Harper's strategic imagination. As one observer concluded, he possessed "a much more expansive sense of what's possible than his predecessors ... he's more Thatcher than Mulroney."[37] In Harper's view, Russia's aggression was not just another example of routine predatory behaviour or, for that matter, a regional adjustment issue. On the contrary, Russia's conduct had wider geopolitical significance, representing a threat to the very foundations of the global order. This belief led him to issue a stark warning to the international community: "All of us who desire peace and stability in the world must recognize that the consequences of these actions will be felt far beyond the borders of Ukraine or even the European continent itself."[38]

Harper understood that, in seizing Ukraine's territory, Russia had demonstrated that the international security assurances, which Ukraine had received early on in exchange for giving up its nuclear arsenal – the Budapest agreements – carried little weight. The political implications were immediately apparent: Russia's actions "provided a rationale for those elsewhere who needed little more encouragement than that already furnished by pride or grievance to arm themselves to the teeth."[39] In invading Ukraine, Putin had made the world a more dangerous and unpredictable place. It was but a short distance for the prime minister to move from simply supporting the status quo to professing his ardent support for the US as system leader.

The strength of Harper's support for US leadership, however, also ironically imposed constraints that limited the scope of Canada's response. While the prime minister was inclined to support Ukraine in its desire to acquire arms, he nonetheless recognized that it would have been imprudent for Canada to do so without the express support of the US. In Washington, the cautious Obama administration – susceptible to mounting criticism of its roles in Libya and Syria – would signal the parameters of the coalition's position by refusing to grant Ukraine's requests for kinetic assistance, arguing that Ukrainian security was better served by pursuing reforms. With the US-led coalition adhering to this policy preference, the Harper government had no choice but to follow suit, since the situational imperatives associated with alliance membership precluded unilateral Canadian action.[40] Had Harper elected to act alone and supply Ukraine with lethal weaponry, it would have signalled disunity among the coalition partners and exposed Canada to the risk of isolation.

Prime Minister Harper regarded the retreat of American leadership under President Obama as a significant geostrategic risk and viewed US retrenchment as a key factor that had emboldened Vladimir Putin to act against Ukraine.[41] Accordingly, the prime minister sought to confront and isolate Russia politically. However, it was Harper's moral universalism that informed his uncompromising position and confrontational approach, explaining his disdain for the policies of accommodation that Canadian governments had pursued throughout the Cold War. It would also account for his interpretation that such policies were naive, immoral, and even dangerous. The horrors of the Second World War, he stated, "could have been avoided" had it not been for political leaders at the time "deliberately turning a blind eye" to the rising threat of Nazi Germany.[42]

Taking a strong ethical stand, then, was not only good politics, but necessary as well. In certain quarters, this certainty of conviction was welcomed given the cynicism and ambiguity associated with retail politics. Indeed, those who lauded Harper's capacity to differentiate between "good and evil," and willingness to confront threats, applauded his "principled stand." His inclination to speak to this dichotomy was seen as evidence of "moral clarity," particularly necessary during times of pressing change and dangerous threats. Sharing the prime minister's view that Canada should not compromise on issues of political and ethical importance, John Baird would fervently proclaim: "A global Canada is a clear-eyed one."[43]

Significantly, Stephen Harper's outlook caused him to be suspicious of the centre-left's moral relativism and neutrality.[44] He objected to the indifference that had seeped into Canada's political discourse, which, in his view, had so enervated the country's past foreign policy practice. Consequently, those who responded to Russia's aggression with moral ambiguity or equivocation became targets of the prime minister's scorn and derision.[45] According to the prime minister, leadership required making "hard choices" to ensure that justice prevailed. From this perspective, the anti-Americanism that characterized Canada's foreign policy past undermined the America's role as system leader. In Harper's view, Canada had a political obligation to support any state that was committed to defending the international liberal order's foundational principles and values. While this obligation certainly extended to the US, it also encompassed any other ally that was willing and able to contribute to the defence of those shared values.[46] Ukraine's democratic aspirations placed it squarely within this camp.

In a major foreign policy speech in 2014, Stephen Harper spoke to many of the themes that had framed much of his aspirational thinking about Canada's place in the world and what needed to be done to secure it.[47] In his remarks, Harper criticized past governments for their complacency and indifference, for allowing tyrants to go unpunished, and for leaving those championing freedom, democracy, and human rights to feel either abandoned or isolated. In this regard, he was resolute in his belief that Canada needed to play a prominent role in defending freedom everywhere. This, he felt, was "at the heart of what it means to be Canadian," explaining why "Canada [stood] proudly, resolutely, and unequivocally with the people of Ukraine." In this sense, for Harper, Canada's support for Ukraine was not simply a strategic imperative – it was a moral one as well.

The Harper government's Ukraine policy reflected the prime minister's moral certitude, which led him to confront and rebuke President Putin at the 2014 G20 summit in Brisbane, Australia, warning him, "you need to get out of Ukraine." Occurring within a traditionally demure setting of roundtable talks, the incident, startling in its forcefulness, was meant to communicate in no uncertain terms what was expected of Russia, while serving to establish with Canada's coalition partners the unconditional nature of the Canadian position. More to the point, the comment succinctly encapsulated the prime minister's unwavering support for the values of freedom and self-determination as enshrined in the principle of sovereignty.[48] It was the prime minister's position to see that states threatening international peace and security would not be left unopposed and that Canada would be undeterred in its support for a rules-based order – a political responsibility and moral duty from which he, personally, would not balk.

Talk, of course, was one thing, but action an entirely different matter. In the initial phase of the crisis, the symbolic measures and rhetoric masked the meagre assistance provided. Although Canada, along with other coalition partners, had imposed economic sanctions on entities and travel bans on those individuals responsible for Russia's actions, supporters of Ukraine saw these as insufficient. They appealed to the Harper government to supply defensive arms and urged Canada to impress upon the coalition the importance of acting more forcefully against Russia, especially after renewed fighting led to the collapse of the Minsk I agreement and ceasefire.[49] Critics, on the other hand, simply called out the prime minister for being disingenuous in view of the government's cuts to both the defence budget and democracy-building initiatives. The rhetoric, they claimed, did not match Canada's record, concluding that the Harper government's foreign policy approach was either a giant muddle or politically cynical.[50]

Yet, such criticisms, when applied to the Ukrainian crisis, tended to minimize both the impact of alliance considerations and the technical, logistical, and legal difficulties that complicated Canada's ability to provide military assistance, even of the nonlethal variety. More to the point, however, Stephen Harper was adamant the crisis was a "wake-up call" that required that Canada adjust its strategic outlook. And, to the degree that he was convinced Ukraine was in peril, the evidence would show Harper pushed vigorously to ensure that bilateral, non-military aid got through. In the process, it also demonstrated a personal level of commitment that was exceptional.[51]

The Ukrainian crisis had become a touchstone, both for the government and for Stephen Harper. With ideology at the core of his worldview, the prime minister's stance toward Russia hardened. Although he did not believe that the Cold War had returned, he was convinced that "the Cold War has never left Vladimir Putin's mind."[52] Some observers found his assessments unnecessarily pessimistic and grim. Others simply found his slavishness to American goals and ideological inflexibility objectionable. Paul Heinbecker, Canada's former ambassador to the UN, for instance, would take umbrage with this new orientation in Canada's foreign policy, which he claimed harmed Canada's reputation and interests. He would describe the Harper foreign policy as one of "pinched vision, shrunken ambition and political cynicism masquerading as principle."[53]

Heinbecker's criticism dismissed the prime minister's deep emotional response to the crisis as unsophisticated and ingenuous. For Harper, however, support for Ukraine was not an abstract exercise. Time and again, he would argue: "Our steadfast support for the people of Ukraine is not a just a matter of integrity and ideals. It is not just a matter of politics or statecraft. For us this is not even a matter of foreign affairs ... this is personal to Canadians."[54] As he acknowledged, the stakes were high. And although on the face of it the conflict with Russia was about Ukraine, it was also about more than that. The close connection between Canada and Ukraine stemmed from an appreciation of the very values for which Ukrainians were fighting, values that Harper believed Canadians understood intuitively. Canada, he felt, had a moral obligation to support all those who would defend their independence and democracy. Referring to President Putin's query as to why Canada cared so much for Ukraine given that it was "a long way away," the prime minister answered: "Freedom, democracy, justice: this is what Ukrainians want." He would add that this "is at the heart of what it means to be Canadian."

The prime minister's declarations may have struck certain observers as quaint platitudes, empty of substance. But as Stephen

Harper explained: "Today, our foreign policies are informed by our highest values." Taking seriously the notion that "politics is a moral undertaking," he was persuaded that principles had to guide political decisions if only because they helped create certainty in the ambiguous world of politics. Since, as he believed, Canadians were guided by principle, Canada would always be on the side of "right." To this he would confidently add that Canada "may not be Ukraine's most powerful friend but we will always be its most certain." As for Canada's continuing commitment, and believing that Canadians understood what was at stake, the prime minister was unequivocal in stating that they could be counted upon to help. "Whatever lies ahead, Canada and Ukraine will continue to move forward together, confident that our shared dreams and aspirations are right, just and good."[55]

In the end, values, principles, and moral obligation complemented Stephen Harper's strategic outlook, and these were reflected, in turn, in his government's policy measures and statements throughout the crisis. Moreover, as a proposition that spoke to important elements of Canada's history, political culture, and identity, it was difficult to argue against and explained how and why the government's principled support for Ukraine did not generate criticism from the ranks of the parliamentary opposition. All the party leaders agreed that Russia's aggressive actions were unacceptable. More to the point, the Liberal leader Justin Trudeau, backing the government's position, indicated there was unanimity between the two. Thomas Mulcair, leader of the New Democratic Party, also stated that with respect to the crisis, he and the prime minister were both "of one mind." Where there was disagreement, it was largely confined to policy details – the NDP, for example, arguing the government's sanctions list be expanded.[56]

In part, the all-party consensus echoed majority public support for Canada's position on the Ukrainian crisis, suggesting that a values-based foreign policy approach resonated with Canadians. On this point, Liberal MP Chrystia Freeland – later foreign minister under the Trudeau government – recognized that the conflict spoke to more than Ukraine's fate. It was, in her opinion, intimately connected to the fortunes of democracy. "Democratic values are rarely challenged as directly as they are being today in Ukraine." Freeland was adamant: "Their victory will be a victory for us all; their defeat will weaken democracy far from the Euromaidan. We are all Ukrainians now."[57]

The Conservatives under Stephen Harper, of course, were of the same view. But what distinguished them was their contention that Canadians not only intuitively understood the nature of the threat, but also, having historically fought to preserve democracy in the past, would, if called upon, do so again. It was a level of commitment not evident in the case of the Liberals or NDP. Stephen Harper's declarations, in this sense, were in perfect keeping with the popular if not idealized view of Canada as a fighting country that stood for both right and good. As for the Conservatives in general and Stephen Harper in particular, they were utterly convinced that confronting Russian aggression was not simply a strategic necessity but a moral one as well – one around which the majority of Canadians would rally.

CONCLUSION

Neoclassical realism suggests that political leaders perceive systemic stimuli through a combination of lenses. This includes worldview, which can and often does play a role in determining the strategic thinking and policy preferences of foreign policy executives, influencing how they react to international developments. In this instance, worldview conditioned Stephen Harper's understanding of the Ukrainian crisis and injected vigour into the decision-making process. It led him to conclude that the existing international political arrangement and its underlying principles had to be defended as a first-order imperative. It also pushed Canadian foreign policy in a specific direction, drawing attention to the issue of strategic outlook in an age where new and diverse threats coincided with older, more familiar dangers.

All of this, of course, points to the importance of political agency. But agency in this case was not a matter of free will. It was a function of an elite socialization process, which resulted in the new conservatives of Canada (in contrast to their Laurentian counterparts) becoming more receptive to American leadership. In comparison to the prevailing attitude among the Laurentian elites, Harper and his conservative colleagues were unreservedly pro-American. They championed America's central role in maintaining the liberal order and embraced the vision that informed Washington's foreign policy goals in the post–Cold War era. Amid the most serious crisis since the end of the Cold War, there was, of course, opportunity for Laurentian-style constraint. However, for both ideological and strategic reasons, the Harper government consciously pursued a vigorous policy, which, at its core, was distinctly un-Laurentian in its aims and purpose.

This orientation mirrored Stephen Harper's confidence in both the appropriateness and necessity of the US's leadership and global agenda, especially in view of growing international pressures. It further reflected his view that Canada's strong support for this agenda was essential to the short-term stability of the rules-based order upon which so much depended. Accordingly, in tone and tenor, his reaction was neither quiet nor restrained. Rather, he was fulsome and frank in his opposition to Russia's attempt to alter the international order, which threatened to disrupt the peace and stability of the post–Cold War era.

It was a perspective, however, that also gave credence to the idea that the defence of the international order was not simply a strategic imperative, but a moral one as well. Freedom and rights, historically, were at the centre of humanity's long struggle for dignity. Insofar as the liberal project advanced these values, there was, at least from the prime minister's perspective, a consuming obligation to support and defend them. Moreover, the lessons of history taught that only the robust defence of these values could prevent a reversal of history's gains. Ukraine was on the front line of this struggle, and its fate was linked to that of democracy itself. Invoking images around Canada's military past, the prime minister was convinced that Canadians understood that democracy and freedom needed to be protected.

Prime Minister Harper felt that Canadians would not break faith because these were values that defined the experience of being Canadian. It was a perspective that tapped into a widely held narrative about Canada's national identity and reflected his own understanding about the need to defend a cause both right and just. That this was tied to the idea of an international order under threat further persuaded him that the Ukrainian crisis was of national interest and, by extension, a matter of importance to Canadians. Canadians would not turn away, forsaking their interests. Canadians would not turn away and forsake their interests any more than they would deny their basic identity.

5

Stephen Harper's Ukraine Policy: Toward an Understanding

The Harper government's Ukraine policy was shaped by the seriousness of the threat posed by Russia. Russia's annexation of Crimea and its aggression in the Donbas were not simply an attack against Ukraine; such actions fundamentally threatened the core precepts of the liberal international order. In this sense, Ukraine had become a central venue for the defence of the international political system, and its fate had implications that extended far beyond the immediate conflict. Indeed, Canada and the wider coalition were forced to re-evaluate their goal of consolidating the liberal order that had been central to Western strategy since the end of the Cold War. In judging the Russian threat to be acute, the coalition deemed a return to a Cold War–style defence to be the most appropriate course of action. This decision appeared justified. In 2014, the post–Cold War interlude had abruptly come to an end with Russia's actions, giving rise to a new period of danger and uncertainty.

Canada's longstanding position as a status quo power provided a strong strategic incentive to participate in the coalition's efforts sanctioning Russia for its belligerence. Moreover, to the degree that the stability of the liberal international order was at stake, Canada's interests in managing the crisis and in participating in that effort by following the US as system leader were one and the same. Simply observing from the sidelines would have amounted to a tacit admission that the business of maintaining the international order fell exclusively to the major powers. Canadian governments had long rejected any such notion, recognizing that an order shaped solely by the preferences of the major players could possibly entail untenable costs. This said nothing of Canada's status within important multilateral institutions such as NATO and the G7, which would have been critically undermined.[1] Given the degree to which US leadership played a role in setting the global agenda since 1945, a decline in Canadian influence with America would almost certainly have precipitated a loss of influence with its other coalition partners and correspondingly less say over outcomes.

As was the case throughout the Cold War, Canada's strategy of reciprocating by following the US was as necessary as it was expected. The most striking aspect of Canada's foreign policy posture during the Ukrainian crisis, however, was not that it followed the American lead, but rather the degree to which it did so. No less conspicuous was how the Canadian response diverged from those of its NATO allies, which possessed similar influence and power. While differences were most evident at a rhetorical level, there were also other dissimilarities. Canada's overt bilateral measures in support of Ukraine's state institutions and economy were noteworthy, as was its humanitarian aid. No less important was Canada's military assistance and its avid participation in OSCE and NATO missions in Ukraine and Eastern Europe.

Canada's contributions during the crisis were unquestionably significant. In this regard, Canada would have more in common with the US than any of its NATO partners.[2] The strength of the response, of course, speaks to the nature of the threat, which endangered the post-1945 international order. Yet, was the situation now any less acute than when crises erupted during the Cold War – a time when the Canadian preference was to support the status quo unconditionally as a coalition partner? So, why such a forceful stance now?

Canada's uncharacteristic response suggests that systemic imperatives alone do not fully account for its behaviour. Could other second-tier considerations have influenced the policy process and the actions taken? Neoclassical realism invites us to consider a more nuanced and rigorous account of foreign policy making. While placing a premium on the perils facing the international order, it considers the dynamic process whereby factors at other levels combine to reinforce the urgency of the moment, generating the fervency behind Canada's strategic response. But how precisely did this occur?

Spurred by a shifting balance of power, the Ukrainian crisis signalled the return of a confrontational, high-stakes great power competition, generating risk and uncertainty for all parties. Conventional wisdom, of course, has it that Canada felt compelled to follow its foreign policy interests by attempting to mitigate such dangers. But neoclassical realism also makes clear that the advantage or benefits derived from decisions taken are not random; constraints and incentives often shape their content. Consequently, the absence of political constraints at the domestic level would play a role in the Harper government's response. Both the Conservatives' majority mandate and the strong public support for Ukraine during the crisis, for example, were important.[3] Furthermore, Canada's parliamentary opposition was inclined to accept and follow the government's lead, given their shared understanding of the threat. Canada's limited trading relationship with Russia was just as significant, mitigating the possibility of economic blowback. The lack of constraints allowed the Harper government greater policy latitude. However, this still does not explain the forcefulness of the response.

Incentives, as opposed to constraints, are potentially more revealing. The claim that the Harper government's robust backing of Ukraine had the ability to increase its electoral standing among the Ukrainian-Canadian community is frequently cited as a crucial factor. Yet, electoral interests, arguably, had little effect. Indeed, there is nothing to suggest that a quid pro quo was at work; rather, the connections that did exist were largely relational and contingent on overlapping interests between the government and community. Moreover, political reciprocity could not be guaranteed given the pluralist nature of the Ukrainian-Canadian community. In effect, there was little to no electoral advantage for the Harper government to prioritize the Canada-Ukraine relationship, especially as this would have invited recurring pressure from this constituency.

If there was motive, however, it was to reassert Canadian values as a political priority, positioning Canada squarely in defence of a liberal order that historically provided for peace and stability. The defence of values, in effect, served to mobilize opinion during the Ukrainian crisis, linking the issue to ideas and beliefs considered widely shared by Canadians. In this sense, Canada's response was more than a geostrategic concern. Russia's challenge represented a political test. Was Canada prepared to defend the ideas and values said to be at the heart of its identity and political culture? For the prime minister, the answer was clear. At a public memorial paying homage to Canadian sacrifice during the First World War and alluding to present-day challenges, he declared: "But every time that we take to defend the values for which they fought, and for which so many died, we remember their stories in the only way that matters. Justice and freedom; democracy and the rule of law; human rights and human dignity. For a century these are the things for which our fellow citizens fought. And this is the ground on which we will always take our stand."[4]

Values, linked to the conflict, were interpolated as a political interest. But how to translate this, practically speaking, into actions that would not only complement Canada's commitment to a normative, democratic foreign policy framework, but also would work in tandem with its alliance commitments and demonstrate Canadian resolve? This was no easy task. US concerns, for example, had to be accommodated. Indeed, even if the Harper government had been inclined to support Ukraine with arms, this would not have been likely without coalition consensus or, at the very least, American approval. Nevertheless, Canada's lead on the sanctions regime and its other contributions – the use of symbolic measures, support for governance and economic reforms, funding for electoral monitoring and OSCE missions, humanitarian relief, and military training – were all notable in their meaning. The point of these efforts, which were significant, was to establish in the public mind what was at stake and to connect these to the notion that Canada needed to be firm in assisting Ukraine in its struggle and moment of need. By helping Ukraine, the principles that defined the international order, and which resonated with

Canadians as common values, were reasserted. In doing so, support for Ukraine was elevated to the level of national interest.[5]

For the Ukrainian-Canadian community, long committed to the goal of Ukrainian independence, the crisis underscored the difficult circumstances under which Ukraine's post-Soviet transition was taking place. The community reacted to Russian aggression because of its ancestral connection. But it also did so with principle in mind. Russia, through its actions, threatened the post–Cold War order and the peace that had accompanied it. From this perspective, the community and the Harper government shared similar concerns. What brought the two closer, however, was the knowledge and understanding that by depriving Ukraine of its sovereignty, Russia threatened freedom everywhere. For the diaspora, which principally viewed the issue of Ukraine as one of freedom, this represented a political challenge of the first order – an existential threat, the urgency of which community members sought to convey. Consequently, and in keeping with Canadian values, it also set in motion the community's effort to augment the work of a government that was similarly inclined to help by providing aid and assistance.

Significantly, casting values in the role of a national interest – a conscious political act – would imply that agency was also at work here. What, then, are we to make of leadership as a foreign policy determinant? Canadian prime ministers play a role in shaping a government's strategic outlook, policy preferences, and threat assessments, if only because they sit at the apex of the foreign policy–making apparatus. Moreover, as political leaders, they often demonstrate exceptional ability in imprinting themselves on both the parties and the governments they lead. Having survived in power long enough, several prime ministers have earned this distinction, including Stephen Harper, who, as a singular agent of socialization on the Canadian right, and on the basis of his personal experiences and beliefs, gave particular meaning and focus to his decisions while in office.[6]

In particular, Stephen Harper's policies and approach bore the imprint of a worldview that embodied his Reform Party roots.[7] His support for free markets, for small government, and for rights and freedoms were consistent with the Western Canadian brand of populist conservatism that found its original voice within the Reform movement. Reform's enthusiastic embrace of the philosophy of the American political right and the US Republican Party in particular – representing an alternative to the traditional centrism of the Liberals and the progressive Tories alike – the so-called Laurentian consensus – also resonated with him. Through a process of elite socialization, and as a politician committed to refurbishing conservatism in Canada, he would guide its transformation, its eventual reunification, and, ultimately, its ascent to power.[8] But more directly, having received his political education within this Western Canadian and distinctly un-Laurentian milieu, Harper would apply the ideas and lessons learned.

Elite socialization – involving the acceptance and internalization of both America's vision of world order, strategic outlook, and values – had a marked effect on Canadian foreign policy, especially after Stephen Harper assumed political office. Nurtured by Harper, the un-Laurentian consensus that emerged was not simply a reaction against Laurentian hegemony – it also served as a coherent alternative to Canada's orthodox approach to foreign policy. This had important policy implications within the context of the Ukrainian crisis. Specifically, for Prime Minister Harper, it was evident that political resolve was required to deal with the Russian threat. However, being an established skeptic regarding international institutions and the role Canada could play in them, he directed Canada's strategic response along a different course.[9]

Traditional attitudes within Canada's foreign policy establishment, of course, persisted about the continuing relevance of an internationalist approach, but these were checked by arguments outlining the imperatives associated with preserving the existing order.[10] In Harper's view, the threat posed by Russia was both real and pressing, and Canada's orthodox approach to foreign policy making was incapable of meeting that threat. Long suspect of Canada's Liberal-dominated foreign policy, he believed it would be naive to assume that a non-confrontational strategy would placate hostile adversaries. Moreover, it was irresponsible to ignore the wayward behaviour of aggressors, or abandon those who were fighting for the same rights and freedoms that Canadians enjoyed. Canada's traditional foreign policy orientation, which Stephen Harper styled as "going along to get along," could no longer be excused or condoned.[11] To this end, he chided Laurentian elites for having historically prioritized internationalism while sacrificing Canada's national interests in the process. He also cast doubt on the wisdom of relying on an overt strategy of multilateralism. Cooperation, he argued, was a means to an end, not an end unto itself.[12]

However, by rejecting Canada's traditional political approach to foreign policy (and the perspectives underpinning it), the Harper government raised an important question. What then should inform Canada's new foreign policy ethic? Historical parallels proved instructive in this regard. Appeasement of the kind that led to the Second World War was one of history's important lessons. The Munich Agreement opened the road to Nazi aggression, which might have been averted had sufficient resolve been shown at the time. History, in this instance, helped galvanize the prime minister's strategic thinking and preferences, leading him to recognize the importance of backing responsible US leadership with strong Canadian followership. It also led him to conclude that firm resistance was needed to deal with malevolent actors.

The Harper government's strong inclination to defend the international order and follow the US was conditioned by the prime minister's strategic assessment of the imperatives associated with global security and stability. But this assessment was also taking place within a period of US retrenchment, which meant that Harper's strategic imagination was tinged with uncertainty. Convinced of the centrality of the US role, which was in retreat, he would react both by bolstering the coalition as much as possible and by reconceiving the meaning of the global order's defence as a national interest. But he would also work within parameters delineated by a cautious Washington, which looked to contain and not exacerbate the conflict. To this end, Canada's support focused on participating in a sanctions regime and contributing to the collective security initiative in Eastern Europe.

For vocal supporters of Ukraine, these initiatives were less than what was hoped for. As a result, they pushed for more.[13] Intervention and lethal arms, they argued, were needed. Strategic considerations, of course, favoured the arming of Ukraine. Yet, the prospect of escalation was real, and alliance constraints brought their own pressures. Canada, consequently, would resist the community's appeals. In the process, however, Canada increased its bilateral efforts, strengthening Ukraine's economy and governance capacity by delivering funding and expertise while providing non-lethal military assistance and, later, substantial training. These strong bilateral overtures were to be expected if only because the Harper government still, somehow, had to signal that Ukraine was of both strategic and political importance as a stage upon which a struggle for democracy was being conducted. To this effect, the measures taken were intended to persuade coalition allies and Canadians alike that the danger posed by Russia was real.

Overall, Stephen Harper's strategic assessment of the crisis shaped Canada's response. However, the prime minister's interpretation of the crisis also derived its meaning from how it meshed with other aspects of his worldview. Indeed, the jeopardy posed by Russia was not that it simply presented a material risk to global security; rather, according to Stephen Harper, it endangered the very principles underpinning the international order and tested the political capacity of the coalition to defend what it valued most. Guided by the idea that the coalition's strategic interests aligned with values embedded in Canadian political culture, he would assert: "Our commitment to values has never wavered. It is why today, we stand once again beside friends and allies whose sovereignty, whose territorial integrity – indeed, whose very freedoms and existence – are still at risk."[14] Here, political priorities reinforced the prime minister's strategic assessment and hardened his determination to mount a forceful response and to side strongly with the US-led coalition in defence of the international order. The downing of the civilian Malaysia Airlines flight MH17 by Russian-backed insurgents over the skies of eastern Ukraine, with its attendant loss of innocent lives, only served to strengthen his resolve to stand firm in the face of aggression and defence of principles.[15]

But this defence also spoke more deeply to Harper's ideological beliefs, as his political education and acculturation occurred within the context of the Reform movement. As a conservative, liberty, rights, and rule of law were sacrosanct. This was the basis of responsible government and legitimate rule. To deny these was to reject democracy and invite coercion and repression in its stead. In this regard, the history of the twentieth century was a reminder of the costs incurred when democratic principles and values were forsaken. Moreover, marked by endless ideological conflicts, the twentieth century stood as evidence that democracy, as a political system, was frequently under siege by authoritarian regimes and figures that sought democracy's ruin. "They all have one thing in common: the destruction of human liberty," Harper would declare unequivocally.[16]

Stephen Harper believed that the crisis in Ukraine was an expression of the ongoing historical challenge to democratic rule. Moreover, a new ideological battle regarding the form and purpose of government was shaping up. In this regard, the "illiberal democracy" of Putin's Russia represented an existential threat, but also a test.[17] Would the coalition, and Canada, rise to meet the challenge, reaffirming their belief in democracy? Harper was convinced that democracy would triumph, but this required "clarity" of purpose and resoluteness of mind among those who valued rights and freedoms. The order's foundational principles had to be defended if democracy was to survive. Accordingly, the prime minister sought to place Canada within the wider political and historical effort to protect these ideas, which undergirded the global liberal order and with which Canadians identified. The result, however, was an ideologically defined politics, which made for a point of view that was at once determined, combative, and even unapologetic.

Russia's aim to undo the entire postwar liberal project reinforced Stephen Harper's strategic and ideological interpretations of the crisis. It also reinforced his sense of moral duty. His was a worldview that underlined the dangers and risks of a world in turmoil, the fear of which he offset by the obligation to defend and preserve the existing order.[18] Freedom, democracy, and justice helped to define humanity's progress, establishing the standards for good governance while producing the conditions under which a responsible citizenship could take place. But this was possible only because there were those who were willing to fight and die for such values. From Stephen Harper's perspective, democracy, freedom, and justice were hard-won and under constant threat – but worthy of those who would sacrifice everything for them. It made compelling the argument for their defence, especially as it represented, according to Harper, the moral underpinning of a meaningful politics.[19]

From Harper's point of view, in a world full of danger and risk, it was both good and right to defend democracy and the other values that defined the moral content of the liberal order. It was particularly poignant, therefore, that Harper, during his visit to Kyiv on behalf of Canada at the height of the Euromaidan, would pay his respects to the fallen dead at a makeshift memorial. There, he honoured those who sacrificed everything, believing they had died for a just cause and for all those who had faith in freedom.[20] Their example would resonate with a prime minister who was no less heartened by the idea that Canadians in the past had defended democracy and freedom, and would do so again if called upon. Accordingly, Stephen Harper would not in good conscience turn away from the crisis in Ukraine. For him, freedom, justice, and democracy as political undertakings represented both a political interest and a moral duty to defend. In keeping with this understanding, Canada, at the prime minister's direction and insistence, would respond vigorously to Russia's challenge.

∽

The Canadian response to the Ukrainian crisis would represent a defining moment in the Harper government's foreign policy legacy and a notable chapter in Canada's foreign policy history. Central to this dynamic, of course, was Russia's seizure and annexation of the territory of its neighbour. Its actions proved to be the catalyst behind a swift and definitive reorientation in Canadian foreign policy. Pivoting away from the post–Cold War policy of system consolidation, the Russian challenge prompted among coalition members a Cold War–style strategy of system defence. In Canada's case, this assumed a forceful character. This followed because of both the conditions under which the crisis occurred and the prime minister's appreciation of the meaning and significance of the crisis to the international order and Canadian interests.

This redirection suggested a departure from Canada's foreign policy past. However, by favouring a strategy that looked to reinvigorate a coalition prepared to defend a system that had been in place since 1945, there was, in fact, continuity. Informed by global change and its implications for Canadian interests, Canada's foreign policy would return to traditional concerns, reconnecting with a longstanding feature of its foreign policy tradition – preserving the status quo. From this perspective, a different prime minister probably would have reacted to the crisis in a similar manner. Canada's historical commitment to a values-based foreign policy may even have provided further grounds for doing so. This underscores the unanimity that existed between the party leaders, pointing again to continuity. Yet, it was Stephen Harper who was at the leadership helm. Confronted by international uncertainty and focusing on core Canadian interests defined as values, Harper, drawing on his political beliefs and moral convictions, would shape Canada's foreign policy in a manner that would be resolute, unyielding, and, above all, distinctive in its forcefulness.

The threat posed by Russia, of course, remains. Canada's commitment to defending the rules-based order suggests that it will continue to participate in the coalition effort to sanction Russia for its actions. This will also be the case as long as Canadian political culture remains at the centre of Canada's foreign policy identity. Leadership, too, will matter. But there is no indication that the fervour and urgency of Canada's response to the Ukrainian crisis, so apparent under Stephen Harper, will be the "new normal." Indeed, it remains an open question whether a leader who shares

Harper's moral convictions and strategic imagination will once more assume the helm of Canadian foreign policy. Yet, as long as there persists among Canadians the belief in the value of a liberal peace, then a strategic assessment of the Ukrainian crisis and an appreciation of its meaning for international security and Canadian interests may continue to rouse the imagination of Canadian leaders and compel Canada to stand alongside Ukraine in defence of a liberal order, its principles, and ideals. Or, as Canada's minister of defence, Rob Nicholson, put it, foreshadowing the possible length of the conflict in Ukraine, and the strength of Canadian resolve: "We are not going to let up on this ... Whether it takes five years or fifty, the people of Ukraine deserve the freedom that they fought for. That has to be one of our goals."[21]

The Harper Government's Response to the Ukrainian Crisis: A Chronology

DECEMBER 2013

On 4 December, John Baird, minister of foreign affairs, met in Kyiv with Ukraine's opposition leaders and civil society representatives. Paul Grod, president of the Ukrainian Canadian Congress, accompanied him. The trip coincided with a meeting of the Organization for Security and Co-operation in Europe (OSCE), held in Ukraine to bring attention to the worsening human rights situation there.

JANUARY 2014

Minister Baird issued a statement of concern on 17 January regarding an anti-protest law issued by the Yanukovych government. Andrew Bennett, Canada's ambassador for religious freedom, also concluded his mission to Ukraine, where he conveyed Canada's strong support for human rights and freedoms.

FEBRUARY 2014

Minister Baird announced on 14 February that supplies and medical aid to Euromaidan activists would be provided through a financial contribution to the International Renaissance Foundation, a Ukrainian nongovernmental organization. On 28 February,

98 Chronology

Baird led a delegation of parliamentarians, community leaders, and officials to Ukraine, where they met with the newly formed provisional government and civil society leaders.

MARCH 2014

With tensions escalating between Russia and Ukraine, on 1 March Prime Minister Stephen Harper held an emergency meeting of key cabinet ministers and telephoned US President Barack Obama to discuss the deteriorating situation in Ukraine. He issued a public statement calling for the immediate deployment of UN and OSCE monitors, and withdrew Canada's ambassador to Russia in protest.

In a joint statement the following day, Harper and other G7 leaders condemned Russia's invasion of Ukraine and announced that they would "suspend participation in activities associated with the preparation of the scheduled G8 Summit in Sochi in June, until the environment comes back to where the G8 is able to have a meaningful discussion." Aiming to increase pressure on Russia, the government also announced that all bilateral military activities were suspended and gave notice that Canada would not participate in the Canada-Russia Intergovernmental Economic Commission. Canadian government representation at the Sochi Paralympics (7–16 March) was also cancelled.

On 3 March, Prime Minister Harper discussed the worsening military situation with Prime Minister Arseniy Yatseniuk. The following day, Ukraine's national flag was raised over Parliament Hill, and on 6 March the prime minister declared Russia's invasion and military support for pro-Russian separatists in Ukraine's eastern territories to be in violation of international law. When Russia sought to alter the status of Crimea by way of a referendum, Canada, in partnership with the G7, immediately declared the move illegal and then, after the plebiscite, announced that it did not recognize the results. To reassert this position, Canada co-sponsored a UN resolution on 27 March affirming Ukraine's sovereignty and independence, and rejecting the Crimea referendum as null and void.

Chronology

At the request of Ukraine's prosecutor general, on 5 March Canada froze the assets of individuals associated with the former Yanukovych government under the Freezing Assets of Corrupt Foreign Officials Act. Eighteen persons were identified under the legislation. To deter further attempts to create conditions of instability in Ukraine (especially by individuals responsible for facilitating or supporting Russia's military actions), Canadian sanctions were expanded on 19 March, with economic sanctions and travel bans imposed on seventeen Ukrainian and Russian officials, and against another fourteen Russian officials and one financial institution, the Rossiya Bank, on 21 March.

On 13 March, Prime Minister Harper announced $220 million in loans and loan guarantees – conditional on a broader International Monetary Fund package – to help stabilize the Ukrainian economy and support its economic and social development. Visiting Ukraine shortly thereafter (22 March), Harper met with the acting president, Oleksandr Turchynov, and Prime Minister Arseniy Yatsenyuk to discuss Canada's economic assistance and pledged $775,000 in support of an OSCE-led political and security monitoring mission. He also paid his respects to those who fell during the Euromaidan Revolution at a makeshift memorial in central Kyiv.

APRIL 2014

On 17 April, Prime Minister Harper committed twenty Canadian Forces staff officers to assist in NATO planning efforts and six Royal Canadian Air Force CF-18 Hornet fighter aircraft as part of Operation Reassurance in Eastern Europe – Canada's contribution in support of NATO's assurance and deterrence measures in Eastern Europe. This was followed by the announcement that HMCS *Regina* would cooperate with NATO's standing maritime forces in the region and that Canadian troops would take part in NATO's Orzel Alert exercise in Eastern Europe. Further sanctions were applied on 12 April against two Russian individuals and a Crimean oil-and-gas company, Chornomornaftogaz, and then on 18 April against nine more individuals and two Russian banks.

MAY 2014

On 12 May, the prime minister announced economic sanctions and travel bans against twelve Ukrainians and Russians. Meanwhile, following up on his government's commitment of 23 April to provide $11 million to support 500 election observers, Harper tasked Senator Raynell Andreychuk and former Ontario premier Mike Harris with leading Canada's mission to Ukraine to monitor the country's May 25 presidential election.

JUNE 2014

Prime Minister Harper attended the inauguration ceremony of Ukraine's new president, Petro Poroshenko – one of the few Western leaders to do so. On 21 June, he announced further sanctions against eleven Russians and Ukrainians, as well as a commercial enterprise in Crimea.

JULY 2014

Canadian aid and assistance to Ukraine remained strong throughout July. Ed Fast, the international trade minister, embarked on a 9–11 July trade and development mission during which he discussed prospects for advancing a Canada-Ukraine free trade agreement, committed $100,000 for Ukraine's Economic Advisory Council, and announced $19.6 million to train farmers as well as facilitate market access and financing for Canadian companies in Ukraine. On 23 July, parliamentary secretary James Bezan and parliamentarian Ted Opitz announced $3.2 million in support of an OSCE project providing human rights training for judges in order to strengthen Ukraine's judiciary and the rule of law. And on 30 July, Christian Paradis, Canada's minister of international development, announced funding of $8.1 million over three years for a new Canadian assistance project, "Strengthening Multi-Party Democracy," designed to strengthen civil society and political pluralism in Ukraine.

The downing of a passenger aircraft, Malaysia Airlines flight MH17, over the Donbas on 17 July – a major international incident – highlighted the volatility and precariousness of the situation in Ukraine. Upon hearing of the attack, the prime minister released a statement expressing dismay and sorrow at the loss of innocent lives. This was followed by a 26 July *Globe and Mail* op-ed – "Our duty is to stand firm in the face of Russian aggression" – penned by the prime minister, as well as a joint G7 statement censuring Russia for its actions in Ukraine. The latter statement insisted on a prompt and unimpeded international investigation into the downing of the airliner.

On the sanctions front, on 11 July the prime minister announced additional economic sanctions and travel bans against fourteen individuals. After the downing of the Malaysian airliner, new sanctions were levied, on 24 July, against eight individuals as well as the Donetsk People's Republic and the Luhansk People's Republic.

AUGUST 2014

On 5 August, parliamentary secretary Lois Brown announced $3.6 million in additional funding for an initiative to overhaul Ukraine's juvenile justice system. Then, on 15 August, she announced a further $3,832,000, over five years, to support an International Finance Corporation project to improve the performance of small- and medium-size agricultural enterprises in Ukraine. Canada imposed additional sanctions on 6 August against nineteen Russian and Ukrainian individuals, and twenty-two businesses and organizations, including the Vostok Battalion and Luhansk Guard paramilitaries.

On 7 August, Prime Minister Harper announced that a Canadian Hercules air transport would deliver non-lethal security assistance to Ukraine. Some two weeks later, on the anniversary of Ukraine's independence, he called on Russia to cease all provocative military activity in Ukraine. To reinforce this message, Canada's minister of foreign affairs issued a statement on 28 August condemning Russia for its ongoing incursions into Ukraine and insisting that Russian forces be withdrawn and the flow of arms ended, including anti-aircraft systems being deployed across the international border.

SEPTEMBER 2014

Early in September, Defence Minister Rob Nicholson announced that Canada's Air Task Force had officially joined NATO's Baltic Air Policing (BAP) mission. Specifically, four CF-18 Hornet aircraft and 130 RCAF personnel would work with NATO allies as part of BAP from September to December 2014, helping to maintain the integrity of the airspace around Estonia, Latvia, and Lithuania.

As part of Operation Reassurance, and underscoring Canada's commitment to working with NATO allies in Central and Eastern Europe, Nicholson made several announcements. Approximately 100 Canadian troops would participate in the NATO exercise Steadfast Javelin II in Latvia (1–8 September), while a small contingent of Canadian soldiers would take part in Rapid Trident 14, a multinational exercise at the International Peacekeeping and Security Centre in Yavoriv, Ukraine (11–28 September). Finally, HMCS *Toronto* would join vessels from several partner nations in the Black Sea as part of an exercise (6–27 September) to enhance maritime security in the region.

Meanwhile, Prime Minister Harper indicated on 4 September that Canada would provide $1 million through NATO trust funds to help upgrade Ukraine's command-and-control capacity and computer and communications capabilities to NATO standards. Additionally, three NATO Centres of Excellence in the Baltic states – Cooperative Cyber Defence, Energy Security, and Strategic Communications – were identified as recipients of $3 million to help deter Russian aggression in the region.

The prime minister also looked to publicize Canada's political engagement with Ukraine. Attending the community-organized "United for Ukraine" gala in support of the Ukrainian-Canadian humanitarian relief effort on 11 September, he announced that

Canada would send short- and long-term observers to help monitor Ukraine's 26 October parliamentary elections. At the event, the prime minister made known that he had received the elections monitoring report produced by Senator Andreychuk and former Ontario premier Harris for the Ukrainian presidential election of 25 May, and announced that Ukraine's president would visit Canada.

On 17 September, Stephen Harper welcomed Ukraine's new president, Petro Poroshenko, and invited him to address the House of Commons and Senate in a rare joint session. The $200 million loan, negotiated earlier, to promote reforms in Ukraine's economic and financial sectors, was finally concluded in a signing ceremony. As a gesture of humanitarian concern and goodwill, the prime minister also announced $3 million in assistance for the estimated 3.9 million people living with violence in the conflict zones and the nearly 200,000 persons internally displaced due to the fighting.

The foreign affairs minister, John Baird, reported on 16 September that sanctions would be imposed on four Russian individuals, five Russian organizations, and one financial institution. He also announced that Canada would send more than 300 observers to monitor Ukraine's parliamentary elections. At the UN on 25 September, together with his G7 counterparts, Baird issued a statement welcoming the Minsk agreement (5 and 19 September). The agreement was seen as an important step toward securing a sustainable ceasefire, safeguarding the Russian-Ukrainian border, and returning to peace in eastern Ukraine.

OCTOBER 2014

On 3 October, parliamentary secretary James Bezan announced $9.76 million in Canadian support, over five years, for "Quality and Accessible Legal Aid," a new project providing legal aid services to the most vulnerable in Ukraine. On a 6–11 October visit to Kyiv and Lviv, Andrew Bennett, Canada's ambassador for religious freedom, announced support for two projects: $950,000 over three years to promote the security of religious and other

104 Chronology

minority communities, and $240,000 over two years for initiatives encouraging religious tolerance and reconciliation. Meanwhile, Defence Minister Nicholson stated on 13 October that HMCS *Toronto* had joined the NATO exercise Noble Justification (13–26 October) as part of Operation Reassurance in the Black Sea, and would also participate in the Turkish-led NATO anti-submarine exercise Mavi Balina in November.

NOVEMBER 2014

Following the reported movement of Russian troops and weapons on the Russia-Ukraine border, the foreign affairs minister, John Baird, issued statements on 5 and 13 November condemning Russia's provocations. The minister also delivered a major speech at the NATO Council of Canada Conference on 18 November, addressing Russia's aggression while reaffirming Canada's support for Ukraine – points he reiterated in a 21 November op-ed in the *Toronto Star*. Meanwhile, on 16 November, Prime Minister Harper met with Herman Van Rompuy, outgoing president of the European Council, and Jean-Claude Juncker, the new president of the European Commission. Together, they emphasized the importance of remaining resolute in the face of Russia's continuing violation of Ukraine's sovereignty and territorial integrity.

On 26 November, Defence Minister Nicholson announced that Canada would provide non-lethal military equipment to the Ukrainian armed forces. The donated gear would include equipment such as tactical communications systems, explosive ordnance disposal equipment, night-vision goggles, medical kits, and winterized clothing.

DECEMBER 2014

Following NATO and OSCE council meetings in early December, Minister Baird, alongside other NATO partners, reaffirmed Canada's commitment and support for Ukraine, and approved a declaration of intent to undertake joint military training and capacity building in Ukraine. Meanwhile, on 19 December Prime Minister

Harper announced economic sanctions and travel bans against an additional twenty Russians and Ukrainians, as well as new export restrictions on technologies used by Russia's extractive sectors.

JANUARY 2015

On 22 January, Minister Baird issued a statement demanding that Russia fully abide by its commitments under the Minsk agreements. This was followed two days later by another statement condemning indiscriminate rocket attacks by Russian-backed separatists on the Ukrainian city of Mariupol'.

On 26 January, Ed Fast, minister of international trade – then on his second trade mission to Ukraine – announced $52 million in support of four initiatives: economic and governance reform in Ukraine, encouraging the development of cooperatives, and promoting sustainable development in the dairy and grain sectors.

FEBRUARY 2015

On 9 February, Prime Minister Harper met with the German chancellor, Angela Merkel, to discuss the international community's response to the crisis in Ukraine. Sanctions were also stepped up in February, with additional measures against thirty-seven Russians and Ukrainians, as well as seventeen entities, mostly paramilitaries. Meanwhile, Defence Minister Nicholson announced on 2 February that Canada would join the US-Ukraine Joint Commission on Defense Reform and Bilateral Cooperation to better coordinate Canada's ongoing assistance to Ukraine's military.

Appointed foreign minister on 9 February, Nicholson issued a statement soon afterward, on 20 February, condemning the ongoing violations of the ceasefire in eastern Ukraine and calling on Russian-backed separatists to acknowledge and quickly implement the terms of the Minsk agreement. On 23 February in Ottawa, Nicholson met with Andriy Parubiy, deputy speaker of the Ukrainian parliament and former secretary of Ukraine's National Security Council, to discuss the country's security needs.

Also, and in the context of an international campaign, Nicholson called upon Russia to immediately end the detention of Nadiya Savchenko, a Ukrainian citizen and combatant in the Donbas conflict, who was engaged in a hunger strike to protest her abduction, ill treatment, and illegal imprisonment in Russia.

MARCH 2015

In early March, Jason Kenney, newly appointed as minister of defence, announced the departure for Eastern Europe of 125 Canadian military personnel from 3rd Battalion, the Royal Canadian Regiment, in support of NATO security assurance measures. He also reported on 5 March that HMCS *Fredericton* had arrived in the Baltic Sea as part of Operation Reassurance and that forty-five Canadian Army personnel would join the multinational NATO training exercise Summer Shield in Latvia (22–31 March).

Minister Nicholson signed an agreement on 27 March regarding the disbursement of Canada's second $200 million low-interest loan to Ukraine to help stabilize the country's economy while supporting programming initiatives consistent with Canadian development priorities. Nicholson added that Canada would contribute $2 million in support of twenty-five Canadian monitors joining the OSCE Special Monitoring Mission to Ukraine.

APRIL 2015

Defence Minister Kenney released a statement regarding the participation of the 3rd Battalion, Royal Canadian Regiment, in the NATO exercise Mountain Warrior, a multinational training opportunity in Poland that would demonstrate Canada's commitment to security in Eastern Europe. The prime minister also announced, on 14 April, the government's intention to provide 200 military personnel to help train and build the capacities of Ukrainian armed forces personnel. This proposal was discussed in a special, four-hour "take note" debate in Canada's House of Commons on 29 April, in which all of Canada's political parties expressed support for the mission.

In attendance at the International Support for Ukraine Conference, on 28 April Chris Alexander, Canada's citizenship and immigration minister, announced the Partnership for Local Economic Development and Democratic Governance, an initiative valued at $19.7 million over six years, which would draw on the expertise and experience of the Federation of Canadian Municipalities. In Ottawa on 29 April, meeting with senior Canadian cabinet officials, Ukrainian foreign affairs minister Pavlo Klimkin discussed aid and technical assistance for Ukraine. Klimkin's Canadian counterpart, Rob Nicholson, responded by announcing $14 million in additional funding for seven projects, including: $8 million to combat human trafficking (implemented by the International Organization for Migration), $3 million for polio immunization (implemented by UNICEF), and $1.6 million for protecting human rights (implemented by the Ukrainian Helsinki Human Rights Union).

MAY 2015

On his 11–12 May trip to Ukraine, Nicholson, Canada's foreign minister, met with President Poroshenko to discuss Canada's assistance programs. In Kyiv, he also visited the central military hospital where Canadian medical volunteers were serving and announced a call, valued at $30 million, for Canadian organizations to help foster the competitiveness of small- and medium-size enterprises in Ukraine. Proposals would be supported through Canada's economic development assistance program. In May, Defence Minister Kenney reported on Canadian involvement in the NATO exercise Sarmis as part of Canada's Operation Reassurance.

JUNE 2015

In Europe for multilateral and bilateral meetings, Prime Minister Harper began with a visit to Ukraine accompanied by Paul Grod, president of the Ukrainian Canadian Congress. In advance of his mission to Europe, Harper stated publicly that Canada was strongly opposed to Russia rejoining the G7. The message was welcomed in Kyiv, where, on 6 June – his third visit to Ukraine since 2014 – Harper officially announced that Canadian negotiators would resume free trade discussions with their Ukrainian counterparts. (The talks had been suspended in September 2013 under the Yanukovych government.) Harper also committed $5 million to help reform Ukraine's police and security sector, and for the deployment of Canadian police trainers under an arrangement with the RCMP. After attending the G7 meeting in Emlau, Germany, where consensus on applying added pressure on Russia was achieved, the prime minister boarded HMCS *Fredericton* in a show of support for naval personnel serving as part of Standing NATO Maritime Group 2, on patrol in the Baltic Sea.

For his part, Defence Minister Kenney met with his NATO counterparts in Brussels (24–25 June) to reaffirm the organization's support for and commitment to defend Ukraine. From Brussels, Kenney travelled to Ukraine, where he visited the International Peacekeeping and Security Centre at Yavoriv, where thirty Canadian observers were stationed, and discussed the proposed expansion in military-technical cooperation between the two countries. He also announced $15 million to support judicial reform and press freedom as means for advancing democratic institution building in Ukraine.

In a parallel development, ninety troops from the 5 Canadian Mechanized Brigade Group were deployed to Poland as part of Operation Reassurance, adding to the contingent already training with Polish forces as part of the NATO exercise Lancer Strike. Toward the end of the month (29 June), under the provisions of the Special Economic Measures (Ukraine) Regulations (contained in the Special Economic Measures Act), Canada prohibited Canadian citizens and anyone living in Canada from conducting any transaction or activity in Crimea.

JULY 2015

On the anniversary of Nadiya Savchenko's illegal detention, Canada's minister of foreign affairs, Rob Nicholson, called again for her release. At the end of the month, he issued a statement condemning Russia's veto of a UN Security Council resolution to create an international tribunal to prosecute those responsible for the downing of Malaysia Airlines flight MH17.

Negotiations for a free trade deal accelerated in June. The deal successfully concluded, Ukraine's Prime Minister Yatseniuk arrived in Canada and, together with Prime Minister Harper, signed the Canada-Ukraine Free Trade Agreement on 14 July, ending (after parliamentary ratification) nearly all import duties on goods traded between Ukraine and Canada.

AUGUST 2015

On the election campaign trail, Stephen Harper issued a statement marking the twenty-fourth anniversary of Ukraine's independence, declaring: "We stand with Ukraine against the Putin regime's aggression."

SEPTEMBER 2015

On 14 September, Canada's Department of National Defence announced the formal start of Canada's field training mission at the International Peacekeeping and Security Centre at Yavoriv and the Ukrainian Ministry of Defense Demining Centre in Kamianets-Podilskyi.

Source: "The Government of Canada's Response to the Situation in Ukraine," Government of Canada website, last modified 29 June 2015, https://www.canada.ca/en/news/archive/2015/06/government-canada-response-situation-ukraine.html.

Notes

INTRODUCTION

1 For a discussion of Canada's relations with Ukraine since independence, see: Bohdan S. Kordan, *Strategic Friends: Canada-Ukraine Relations from Independence to the Euromaidan* (Montreal: McGill-Queen's University Press, 2018).

2 Canada's foreign policy engagement with Ukraine under the Trudeau government has been qualitatively different. It has assumed a more reserved character, despite the strong connection between Canada's foreign minister, Chrystia Freeland, and the community, considered an important factor in Canada's current relations with Ukraine. This reflects Canada's return to a more conventional diplomacy stance – working through multilateral networks and global institutions. Canada's potential participation in a peacekeeping mission for Ukraine is but one example of its interest in playing a more traditional and contained role. On the Trudeau government and its proposal for peacekeeping in Ukraine, see: Tonda MacCharles, "No promises, but lots of talk about Canadian peacekeepers in Ukraine," *Toronto Star*, 9 November 2017, https://www.thestar.com/news/canada/2017/11/09/no-promises-but-lots-of-talk-about-canadian-peacekeepers-in-ukraine.html; and Paul Wells, "A peacekeeping force on the Russia-Ukraine border?," *Maclean's*, 28 November 2017, https://www.macleans.ca/politics/ottawa/a-peacekeeping-force-on-the-russia-ukraine-border/.

Notes to pages 4–14

3 Andrew F. Cooper, *Canadian Foreign Policy: Old Habits and New Directions* (Scarborough, ON: Prentice-Hall, 1997), 110–19.

4 John Baird, for instance, praised Stephen Harper's "moral clarity" in a key foreign policy speech. See: Department of Foreign Affairs, Trade and Development (hereafter DFATD), "Address by Minister Baird to the NATO Council of Canada Conference – Ukraine: The Future of International Norms," 18 November 2014, PCUH Archives, Canada-Ukraine Project.

5 See Joseph Brean, "After a half century of liberal internationalism, Tories have forged a new foreign policy myth," *National Post*, 2 January 2015.

6 For a useful discussion of how leadership conditions the shape and direction of foreign policies, see: Daniel L. Byman and Kenneth M. Pollack, "Let Us Now Praise Great Men: Bringing the Statesman Back In," *International Security* 25, no. 1 (Spring 2001): 107–46.

7 On neoclassical realism, see the editors' introduction in Steven E. Lobell, Norrin M. Ripsman, and Jeffrey W. Taliaferro, eds., *Neoclassical Realism, the State, and Foreign Policy* (Cambridge, UK: Cambridge University Press, 2009), 1–41.

8 See William C. Wohlforth, "Realism and the End of the Cold War," *International Security* 19, no. 3 (October 1995): 102.

9 For a more complete discussion, see: Kordan, *Strategic Friends*, 82–6.

CHAPTER ONE

1 Lobell, Ripsman, and Taliaferro, eds., *Neoclassical Realism*.

2 Denis Stairs, "Challenges and Opportunities for Canadian Foreign Policy in the Paul Martin Era," *International Journal* 58, no. 4 (Fall 2003): 498.

3 As it is used here, the term "conservative" refers to Canada's interest in preserving the resources already under its control and the benefits it receives through the maintenance of the existing liberal order, including security and access to foreign markets. As Denis Stairs suggests, "order is a conservative value and Canada is a conveniently located, property-rich state. That being so, it has no interests that acquisitive acts of disorder can serve." For a further discussion, see: Ibid., 497–8.

Notes to pages 16–21

4 Ronald L. Tammen, Jacek Kugler, Douglas Lemke, Alan C. Stam III, Mark Abdollahian, Carole Alsharabati, Brian Efird, and A.F.K. Organski, *Power Transitions: Strategies for the 21st Century* (New York: Chatham House, 2000), 9.

5 Robert Kagan, *The World America Made* (New York: Alfred A. Knopf, 2012), 99.

6 Yoav Gortzak, "How Great Powers Rule: Coercion and Positive Inducements in International Order Enforcement," *Security Studies* 14, no. 4 (October 2005): 666.

7 Charles A. Kupchan, "The Normative Foundations of Hegemony and the Coming Challenge to Pax Americana," *Security Studies* 23, no. 2 (April 2014): 248.

8 Ibid., 249.

9 As Tom Keating argues, middle powers such as Canada "provide important supports to international order and help sustain international society." Tom Keating, "The Transition in Canadian Foreign Policy through an English School Lens," *International Journal* 69, no. 2 (2014): 171.

10 Cesare Merlini, "The Lonely Architect," *Survival* 54, no. 4 (2012): 158.

11 Tammen et al., *Power Transitions*, 36.

12 These values and principles are enshrined in the Atlantic Charter and other founding NATO documents.

13 Roy Rempel, *Dreamland: How Canada's Pretend Foreign Policy Has Undermined Sovereignty* (Montreal: McGill-Queen's University Press, 2006), 2.

14 Randall L. Schweller and William C. Wohlforth, "Power Test: Evaluating Realism in Response to the End of the Cold War," *Security Studies* 9, no. 3 (March 2000): 83.

15 Wohlforth, "Realism and the End of the Cold War," 119.

16 Schweller and Wohlforth, "Power Test," 93.

17 Ibid., 91.

18 The phrase "end of history" is drawn from Francis Fukuyama's *The End of History and the Last Man*, which is often portrayed uncharitably as an un-nuanced embodiment of post–Cold War liberal triumphalism. For a retrospective discussion of the work and its impact, see the updated version (with afterword): Francis Fukuyama,

114   Notes to pages 22–3

The End of History and the Last Man (New York: First Free Press, 2006): 341–54.

19 The Mulroney government moved in the direction of promoting neo-liberal values during the late 1980s, evidence of which is its formation of the International Centre for Human Rights and Democratic Development (ICHRDD). A division within the Canadian International Development Agency, the ICHRDD was tasked with promoting Western democratic values – including what the government termed "good governance." For a discussion of the Mulroney government's shift toward embracing a more interventionist strain of liberalism, see: Paul Gecelovsky and Tom Keating, "Liberal Internationalism for Conservatives: The Good Governance Initiative," in *Diplomatic Departures: The Conservative Era in Canadian Foreign Policy, 1984–93*, ed. Nelson Michaud and Kim Richard Nossal (Vancouver: UBC Press, 2009): 194–207; and Doug Saunders, "The World Needs Canada Back in the Democracy Export Business," *Globe and Mail*, 29 December 2017, https://www.theglobeandmail.com/opinion/the-world-needs-canada-back-in-the-democracy-export-business/article37454136/.

20 Thomas Keating, *Canada and World Order: The Multilateralist Tradition in Canadian Foreign Policy* (Don Mills, ON: Oxford University Press, 2013), 168.

21 Ibid.

22 Schweller and Wohlforth, "Power Test," 81.

23 For an analysis of the challenges facing the West in the aftermath of the collapse of the USSR, see: Bohdan S. Kordan, *Other Anxieties: Ukraine, Russia and the West* (Kingston, ON: Kashtan Press, 1994), 36–44.

24 Seth Weinberger, "Institutional Signaling and the Origins of the Cold War," *Security Studies* 12, no. 4 (January 2003): 86.

25 On the politics of Ukrainian denuclearization, see: Nadia Schadlow, "The Denuclearization of Ukraine: Consolidating Ukraine's Security," in *Ukraine in the World: Studies in the International Relations and Security Structure of a Newly Independent State*, ed. L. Hajda (Cambridge, MA: Harvard University Press, 1998), 271–87.

26 In international relations, policy makers attempt to decipher whether a state supports or opposes the prevailing regime by monitoring its

behaviour for relevant signals. Likewise, policy makers recognize that the consequences of their own policies depend in part on how those policies are interpreted by other states. The perceived credibility of a signal is strengthened if the costs associated with engaging in the behaviour are great. Some signals are stronger than others, establishing greater levels of certainty and trust, and heightening the prospects for cooperation. See: Weinberger, "Institutional Signaling," 86.

27 The Budapest Memorandum relates to several agreements concluded in December 1994 which provided security assurances, by the Russian Federation, the US, and United Kingdom, relating to the accession of Ukraine, Belarus, and Kazakhstan to the Treaty on the Non-Proliferation of Nuclear Weapons (originally signed in 1968). These assurances were aimed at addressing threats or the use of force against the territorial integrity or political independence of the newly independent states. Specifically, the signatories pledged to refrain from making each other's territory the object of military occupation or engage in other uses of force in violation of international law, and that no such occupation or acquisition of territory would be recognized as legal. France and China gave similar assurances (although somewhat weaker ones) in separate documents.

28 See the discussion in Bohdan S. Kordan, "Canadian-Ukrainian Relations: Articulating the Canadian Interest," *Harvard Ukrainian Studies* 20 (January 1996): 125–44.

29 In this regard, Ukraine's willingness to accept nuclear non-proliferation norms was regarded as a key benchmark measuring its acceptance of the post–Cold War international order. Only when the nuclear issue was resolved did the Canada-Ukraine relationship hit its stride. The events are discussed at length in Kordan, *Strategic Friends*, 41.

30 At an official reception during a 1996 visit to Kyiv by Canada's foreign minister, Lloyd Axworthy, the minister stated, in a toast to his hosts: "Canadians care about your country. We care because we are in your debt. You gave us the talent and energy of your ancestors. And we care for a less sentimental reason – because the success of your independence is in our interest. It is in the peace and stability of Europe for which Canadian have fought twice in this century." Department of Foreign Affairs, Trade and Development (hereafter DFATD), "Toast by Minster Axworthy," 5 June 1996, PCUH Archives, Canada-Ukraine Project.

CHAPTER TWO

1 Norrin M. Ripsman, Jeffrey W. Taliaferro, and Steven E. Lobell, *Neoclassical Realist Theory of International Politics* (New York: Oxford University Press, 2016), 52–7.

2 Tammen et al., *Power* Transitions, 136.

3 The improvements in Russia's situation since 1991 also resulted in part from the benefits it received from its entry into or association with many of the key Western clubs. In addition to gaining membership in the International Monetary Foundation and G8 state grouping in 1992, Russia acceded to the NATO-Russia Founding Act in 1997 and gained full membership in the World Trade Organization in 2012. In each instance, Russia gained greater access to important sites of global governance and increased its global share of valued goods.

4 Critics of this perspective would suggest that it was in fact NATO, the US, and the EU that revised the status quo, ignoring Russia's interest in reestablishing its regional hegemony. This is at the heart of the debates around the origins of the crisis and which party was at fault. For contrasting perspectives, see: Richard Sakwa, *Frontline Ukraine: Crisis in the Borderlands* (London: I.B. Tauris, 2016); and Taras Kuzio, *Putin's War Against Ukraine: Revolution, Nationalism and Crime* (Toronto: CreateSpace Independent Publishing Platform, 2017).

5 Matthew Dalton, "Hollande Offers Sharp Critique of US Policy," *Wall Street Journal*, 12 October 2016, http://www.wsj.com/articles/hollande-offers-sharp-critique-of-u-s-policy-1476287400.

6 David Yost, "The Budapest Memorandum and Russia's intervention in Ukraine," *International Affairs* 91, no. 3 (2015): 513–19.

7 Richard Haas, *A World in Disarray: American Foreign Policy and the Crisis of the Old Order* (New York: Penguin, 2017), 3.

8 For a helpful discussion of the costs and benefits associated with economic sanctions, see: Tammen et al., *Power Transitions*, 116–17.

9 Scholars have noted that there is a strong imperative to prevent a strategic alignment between Russia and China. Such an alignment would have serious consequences for system stability in general and the security of NATO member states in particular. However, developments since 2000 have greatly complicated the task of preventing a

Notes to pages 33–5

strategic alignment between the two great powers. For a discussion of the issue, see: Ibid., 138–52.

10 Robert Kagan traces the beginning of the period of American retrenchment to the beginning of Barack Obama's presidency in 2009. See: R. Kagan, "The Weight of Geopolitics," *Journal of Democracy* 26, no. 1 (January 2015): 21.

11 DFATD, "Backgrounder – Canadian Participation in NATO Reassurance Measures," 3 July 2014; and Office of the Prime Minister of Canada (hereafter PMO), "PM Announces the Extension of Operation Reassurance," 31 July 2015, PCUH Archives, Canada-Ukraine Project.

12 In a 2014 speech, US President Barack Obama alluded to the importance of assembling a broad international coalition in response to Russia's challenge to world order. See: Office of the US Press Secretary, "Remarks by the President in Address to European Youth," 26 March 2014, https://whitehouse.gov/the-press-office/2014/03/26/remarks-president-address-european-youth.

13 "German leader says no to Iraq war," *Guardian*, 6 August 2002, https://www.theguardian.com/world/2002/aug/06/iraq.johnhooper.

14 Andrew Parkin, "Pro-Canadian, Anti-American or Anti-War? Canadian Public Opinion on the Eve of War," *Policy Options*, 1 April 2003, https://policyoptions.irpp.org/magazines/big-ideas/pro-canadian-anti-american-or-anti-war-canadian-public-opinion-on-the-eve-of-war/.

15 Lobell, Ripsman, and Taliaferro, *Neoclassical Realism*, 7.

16 Susan Lunn, "Russian ships track HMCS Fredericton carrying Stephen Harper," *CBC News*, 10 June 2015, https://www.cbc.ca/news/politics/russian-ships-track-hmcs-fredericton-carrying-stephen-harper-1.3107649.

17 Michael Petrou, "It's Time for Tougher Sanctions Against Russia," *Maclean's*, 28 August 2014, http://www.macleans.ca/politics/worldpolitics/two-options-for-the-west-concede-ukraine-to-russia-or-escalate-sanctions/; and Mark MacKinnon, "A divided Western front is playing into Putin's endgame," *Globe and Mail*, 5 February 2015, https://www.theglobeandmail.com/news/world/a-divided-western-front-is-playing-towards-putins-endgame/article22825463/.

18 Tammen et al., *Power Transitions*, 116–17.

118 Notes to pages 36–7

19 Describing the Euromaidan as a "coup" supported by the West, President Vladimir Putin cast Russia's annexation of Crimea as sanctioned under international law after a referendum was quickly organized. Putin claimed that Russia had a right to protect ethnic Russians beyond its borders, citing Kosovo's independence as a precedent for Russia's military intervention. See: The Kremlin, "Address by the President of the Russian Federation," Moscow, 18 March 2014, http://en.kremlin.ru/events/president/news/20603.

20 "'An outrage': World leaders react to Malaysian Airlines MH17," *Global News*, 18 July 2014, https://globalnews.ca/news/1459290/an-outrage-world-leaders-react-to-malaysian-airlines-mh17/; and Josh Wingrove, "MH17: Harper urged to support international probe of Malaysia Airlines crash," *Globe and Mail*, 18 July 2014.

21 PMO, "PM Delivers Remarks at the United for Ukraine Gala," 11 September 2014, PCUH Archives, Canada-Ukraine Project.

22 Ibid.

23 President Barack Obama characterized Russia's aggression against Ukraine in value-laden terms similar to those used by Stephen Harper and other Canadian officials, describing Russia's actions a "challenge to our ideals – to our very international order." See: Office of the US Press Secretary, "Remarks by the President in Address to European Youth."

24 DFATD, "Address by Minister Baird to the NATO Council of Canada Conference – Ukraine: The Future of International Norms," 18 November 2014, PCUH Archives, Canada-Ukraine Project.

25 President Obama characterized Russia as the aggressor, and remarked that its actions in Ukraine "recall the days when Soviet tanks rolled into Eastern Europe." In the same speech, Obama described the US response to the crisis as "standing with our allies on behalf of the international order." See: Office of the US Press Secretary, "Remarks by the President at the United States Military Academy Commencement Ceremony," 28 May 2014, https://obamawhitehouse.archives.gov/the-press-office/2014/05/28/remarks-president-united-states-military-academy-commencement-ceremony.

26 President Vladimir Putin described Russia's actions in the Ukrainian crisis as defensive measures introduced in response to the post–Cold

War expansion of NATO and the European Union, which, he claimed, were engaged in an effort to encircle Russia. He blamed the West for ignoring Russia's security concerns and portrayed the West as the aggressor. See: Kremlin, "Address by the President of the Russian Federation."

27 John Baird, "Russia's Aggression Is Against Its Own Best Interest," *Toronto Star*, 21 November 2014, PCUH Archives, Canada-Ukraine Project.

28 Ibid.

29 "John Baird announces more sanctions against Russia," *CBC News*, 16 September 2014, https://www.cbc.ca/news/politics/john-baird-announces-more-sanctions-against-russia-1.2767872.

30 According to F. Stephen Larrabee, Ukraine's successful integration into the EU and other Western structures would preclude "the restoration of Soviet hegemony in the post-Soviet space." See: F. Stephen Larrabee, "Russia, Ukraine and Central Europe: The Return of Geopolitics," *Journal of International Affairs* 63, no. 2 (April 2010), 48.

31 See: Mark MacKinnon, "Canada does not have right weapons to help Ukraine, Defence Minister reveals," *Globe and Mail*, 25 June 2015, https://www.theglobeandmail.com/news/world/kenney-says-canada-doesnt-have-the-right-weapons-to-give-ukraines-army/article25116785/.

32 Brad Bird, "Why Canada stands with Ukraine and what it is doing to help," *Kyiv Post*, 3 March 2015; and Steven Chase, "Stephen Harper heads to Ukraine, but won't commit to providing weapons," *Globe and Mail*, 5 June 2015, https://www.theglobeandmail.com/news/politics/stephen-harper-heads-to-ukraine-still-wont-provide-weapons/article24816921/.

33 Ukrainian Canadian Congress (hereafter UCC), "Briefing Note to the Government of Canada: The Case for Military Assistance to Ukraine," 3 September 2014, PCUH Archives, Canada-Ukraine Project.

34 Ibid.

35 Bob Onyschuk, "A broken promise to protect Ukraine sovereignty," *National Post*, 12 March 2014, https://nationalpost.com/opinion/bob-onyschuk-a-broken-promise-to-protect-ukraine-sovereignty.

36 UCC, "Briefing Note to the Government of Canada."

120 Notes to pages 41–9

37 For a description of this role, see: Douglas Alan Ross, "Canada's International Security Strategy: Beyond Reason But Not Hope?," *International Journal* 62, no. 2 (spring 2010): 357.
38 Rempel, *Dreamland*, 2.

CHAPTER THREE

1 See: Steven E. Lobell, "Threat Assessments, the State, and Foreign Policy: A Neoclassical Realist Model," in Lobell, Ripsman, and Taliaferro, eds., *Neoclassical Realism*, 62–4.
2 The United Nations did not play a significant role in managing the Ukrainian crisis. This relates in part to the structure of the UN Security Council, where Russia holds a permanent seat. The UN's inaction resulted in other international institutions and multilateral groupings taking the lead, most notably the OSCE, NATO, and the G7.
3 Lobell, "Threat Assessments," 56.
4 Ripsman, Taliaferro, and Lobell, *Neoclassical Realist Theory of International Politics*, 46.
5 Defence of the existing rules-based order is in the collective interest of all status quo powers inasmuch as it allows for the provision of international public goods such as security, free trade, and rule of law. Martin Wight has described the maintenance of international order as a "universal interest." See: Martin Wight as quoted in Tom Keating, "The Transition in Canadian Foreign Policy through an English School Lens," 171.
6 Brean, "After a half century."
7 The Reform Party was critical of Canada's foreign policy direction under both Liberal and Progressive Conservative governments. It viewed both parties as perpetuating a foreign policy orientation that did not adequately reflect the full spectrum of Canada's values. See: Reform Party of Canada, *Platform & Statement of Principles* (1989), 25.
8 The Harper government engaged in a more radical form of politics (in the international relations sense of the term) partly because it embraced an "American style" of liberalism that was classical in nature. For a discussion of this new politics and its implications, see: Adam Chapnick, "Peace, Order, and Good Government: The

'Conservative' Tradition in Canadian Foreign Policy," *International Journal* 60, no. 3 (June 2005): 646–50.

9 As Prime Minister Harper put it, "Canada's greatest asset on the international stage is our unique relationship with the United States – and the fact that we just happen to share values and interests with the world's sole superpower." Quoted in Justin Massie and Stephane Roussel, "The Twilight of Internationalism? Neocontinentalism as an Emerging Dominant Idea in Canadian Foreign Policy," in *Canada in the World: Internationalism in Canadian Foreign Policy*, ed. Heather A. Smith and Claire T. Sjolander (Don Mills, ON: Oxford University Press, 2013), 48. See also: PMO, "Statement by the Prime Minister of Canada in Toronto, Tribute to Liberty Dinner," 30 May 2014, PCUH Archives, Canada-Ukraine Project.

10 Paul Wells, "Why Harper wants to take on the world," *Maclean's*, 25 July 2011, http://www.macleans.ca/uncategorized/why-harper-wants-to-take-on-the-world/.

11 Stephen Harper, quoted in Rob Gillies, "Canada's Harper says Russia can't rejoin G7 with Putin in power," *CBC News*, 4 June 2015, http://www.cbc.ca/news/politics/stephen-harper-says-russia-can-t-rejoin-g-7-with-putin-in-power-1.3101040.

12 Stephen Harper, quoted in Massie and Roussel, "The Twilight of Internationalism?," 47. For a discussion of this Canada-US connection, see: Jean-Christophe Boucher, "The Responsibility to Think Clearly about Interests: Stephen Harper's Realist Internationalism, 2006–2011," in Smith and Sjolander, eds., *Canada and the World: Internationalism in Canadian Foreign Policy*, 60.

13 Governor General of Canada, "Speech from the Throne," 41st Parliament, 2nd Session (2013), http://publications.gc.ca/pub?id=9.511908&sl=0.

14 Massie and Roussel explain the Harper government's strong support for the United States as an example of neocontinentalism, an emergent dominant idea in Canadian foreign policy that they suggest is rooted in the rise of a Canadian variant of neoconservatism. Canadian neoconservatives are said to possess "an unqualified belief in the benefits and benevolence of US hegemony." For a discussion of neocontinentalism and neoconservatism, see: Massie and Roussel, "The Twilight of Internationalism?," 36–49.

122 Notes to pages 51–3

On the issue of support for the US in promoting democracy, a senior official argued that it "advances Canada's interests because it offers the best chance for long-term stability, prosperity, and the protection of human rights." For original quote, see: Jonathan Paquin and Philippe Beauregard, "Shedding Light on Canada's Foreign Policy Alignment," *Canadian Journal of Political Science* 46 no. 3 (September 2013): 633.

15 Paul Wells noted this preoccupation as early as 2011. See: Wells, "Why Harper wants to take on the world."

16 General Rick Hillier, chief of the Canadian Forces Defence Staff under Harper between 2006 and 2008, also described Canada as a "warrior nation."

17 See the discussion in Jeremy Keehn, "Stephen Harper, the Ottawa Attack, and the Question of Canadian Security," *New Yorker*, 23 October 2014, https://www.newyorker.com/news/news-desk/ stephen-harper-question-canadian-security; and Norman Hillmer, "Concluding Thoughts: The Prime Minister of the Few," in *The Harper Era in Canadian Foreign Policy: Parliament, Politics, and Canada's Global Posture*, ed. Adam Chapnick and Christopher J. Kukucha (Vancouver: UBC Press, 2016), 267.

18 The issue of principles as interests is discussed in Martin Goldfarb, "Canada's Principled Foreign Policy: No More Honest Broker," *Policy*, January/February 2014, http://policymagazine.ca/pdf/5/articles/ PolicyMagazineJanuary-February-Goldfarb.pdf.

19 On the evolution of Canada-Ukraine relations during the Harper administration, and especially its ambiguous stance toward Ukraine during its early years, see: Bohdan S. Kordan, *Strategic Friends: Canada-Ukraine Relations from Independence to the Euromaidan* (Montreal: McGill-Queen's University Press, 2018), 82–6.

20 Steven Chase, "Ukraine's flag flown on Parliament Hill," *Globe and Mail*, 4 March 2014, https://www.theglobeandmail.com/news/politics/ ukraines-flag-flown-on-parliament-hill/article17269823/.

21 Lee-Anne Goodman, "Stephen Harper in Kyiv as First G7 Leader to Visit Ukraine," *Huffington Post*, 22 March 2014, http://www.huffingtonpost.ca/2014/03/22/stephen-harper-ukraine_n_5012075.html.

22 Mike Blanchfield, "Ukraine's president thanks Canada for unwavering support in speech at joint session of Parliament," *National Post*, 17 September 2014, http://news.nationalpost.com/news/canada/cana-

Notes to pages 54–5

dian-politics/ukraines-president-thanks-canada-for-unwavering-support-in-speech-at-joint-session-of-parliament.

23 PMO, "Statement by the Prime Minister of Canada on the Results of the Ukrainian Elections," 27 May 2014, PCUH Archives, Canada-Ukraine Project; PMO, "Statement by the Prime Minister of Canada on the Parliamentary Elections in Ukraine," 26 October 2014, PCUH Archives, Canada-Ukraine Project; and The Kremlin, "Address by the President of the Russian Federation."

24 DFATD, "Address by Minister Baird at Foreign Affairs, Trade and Development Canada Headquarters," 27 March 2014, PCUH Archives, Canada-Ukraine Project.

25 Kathryn Blaze Carlson, "Canada recalls ambassador from Moscow for consultation," *Globe and Mail*, 1 March 2014, https://www.theglobeandmail.com/news/national/canada-recalling-ambassador-from-moscow-over-russian-intervention-in-ukraine/article17185805/.

26 Governor General of Canada, "Speech from the Throne," 41st Parliament, 2nd Session (2013), http://publications.gc.ca/pub?id=9.511908&sl=0.

27 As quoted in Mark MacKinnon, "Harper's World: Canada's New Role on the Global Stage," *Globe and Mail*, 25 September 2015, https://www.theglobeandmail.com/news/politics/harpers-world-the-past-and-future-of-canadas-foreignpolicy/article26542719/.

28 DFATD, "Address by Minister Baird."

29 Gerd Schönwälder argues that Canada's status as a moral leader on the world stage has been eroded because the Harper government has neither committed the necessary resources nor possessed the instruments by which to advance a values-based foreign policy. And yet, as the government has made clear, Canada's commitment is measured in capabilities, and these have assumed non-traditional forms such as the use of the military in selected roles. Such roles include missions in Afghanistan, Libya, the Baltic countries, and off the coast of Somalia. For a critical analysis of the Harper government's principled foreign policy, see: Gerd Schönwälder, "Principles and Prejudice: Foreign Policy Under the Harper Government," Centre for International Policy Studies, 24 June 2014, https://www.cips-cepi.ca/publications/principles-and-prejudice-foreign-policy-under-the-harper-government/.

124 Notes to pages 55–9

30 DFATD, "Canada Reaffirms Its Support to Ukraine," 5 August 2014, PCUH Archives, Canada-Ukraine Project; DFATD, "Canada Supporting Entrepreneurs in Ukraine," 15 August 2014, PCUH Archives, Canada-Ukraine Project; and DFATD, "Canada Reaffirms Support for Economic Development and Democratic Governance in Ukraine," 28 April 2015, PCUH Archives, Canada-Ukraine Project.

31 DFATD, "Renewed Negotiations Toward a Canada-Ukraine Free Trade Agreement to Promote Growth and Prosperity in Ukraine," 26 January 2015, PCUH Archives, Canada-Ukraine Project. The resulting agreement, known as the Canada-Ukraine Free Trade Agreement, was eventually ratified under Prime Minister Trudeau's Liberal government and came into effect 1 August 2017.

32 DFATD, "Minister Nicholson Announces Support for Ukrainian Democracy," 18 March 2015, PCUH Archives, Canada-Ukraine Project.

33 PMO, "Restrictions on Technologies used in Russia's Oil Exploration and Extractive Sector," 19 December 2014, PCUH Archives, Canada-Ukraine Project.

34 Armina Ligaya, "Pain caused by sanctions on Russia for 'greater national interest,' Stephen Harper tells Canadian businesses," *Financial Post*, 24 March 2014, http://business.financialpost.com/news/economy/russia-stephen-harper-business/wcm/f8527f78-7b01-44bc-99f6-44755a67cef5.

35 PMO, "Statement by the Prime Minister of Canada Announcing Security Assistance to Ukraine," 7 August 2014, PCUH Archives, Canada-Ukraine Project; PMO, "PM Announces New Canadian Military Contribution in Ukriane," 14 April 2015; and DFATD, "Minister Nicholson Announces New Support for Ukraine's Armed Forces, Canada Delivers Nonlethal Military Equipment," 9 May 2015, PCUH Archives, Canada-Ukraine Project.

36 PMO, "PM Delivers Closing Remarks at the NATO Summit," 5 September 2014, PCUH Archives, Canada-Ukraine Project.

37 A ceasefire protocol, developed by France, Germany, Ukraine, and Russia, was introduced after an earlier agreement, Minsk I, failed to hold. Minsk II, which set out several peacemaking measures to deescalate the conflict, has not been entirely observed. Casualties occur on a weekly basis. By the end of 2018, there were 12,800 to 13,000 officially reported deaths.

Notes to pages 59–61

38 DFATD, "Canada Announces Support for Free and Fair Elections in Ukraine," 16 September 2014, PCUH Archives, Canada-Ukraine Project; and DFATD, "Minister Nicholson Announces Additional Contributions to OSCE's Special Monitoring Mission in Ukraine," 27 March 2015, PCUH Archives, Canada-Ukraine Project.

39 See, for example: Chris Westdal, "Harper, Ukraine and the price of cheap talk," *iPolitics*, 3 April 2014, https://ipolitics.ca/2014/04/03/harper-ukraine-and-the-price-of-cheap-talk/; and Westdal, "Still dreaming of a miracle in Ukraine," *iPolitics*, 17 February 2015, https://ipolitics.ca/2015/02/17/still-dreaming-of-a-miracle-in-ukraine/.

40 David Carment and Joseph Landry, "Transformation, Ambiguity and Reversal: Harper's Foreign Policy Under a Microscope," *Canadian Foreign Policy Journal* 20, no. 2 (2014): 107; and David Carment and Joseph Landry, "Diaspora and Canadian Foreign Policy: The World in Canada," in *The Harper Era in Canadian Foreign Policy: Parliament, Politics and Canada's Global Posture*, ed. Adam Chapnick and Christopher Kukucha (Vancouver: UBC Press, 2016), 212. See also: Stephen Maher, "Conservative 'principled foreign policy' amounts to little more than vote-seeking," *National Post*, 8 March 2015, https://nationalpost.com/news/canada/stephen-maher-canada-foreign-policy.

41 As quoted in Steven Chase, "Ukrainian politician warns Ottawa not to resume ties with Russia," *Globe and Mail*, 23 February 2016, https://beta.theglobeandmail.com/news/politics/leading-ukrainian-politician-warns-canada-not-to-resume-ties-with-russia/article28850712/. For Lavrov's full remarks, see: Ministry of Foreign Affairs of the Russian Federation, "Sergey Lavrov's remarks and answers to media questions at a news conference on Russia's diplomacy performance in 2015," 26 January 2016, http://www.mid.ru/en/vistupleniya_ministra/-/asset_publisher/MCZ7HQuMdqBY/content/id/2032328.

42 Paul Grod, "Canadian values are Ukrainian values," *Embassy*, 9 June 2015, http://www.embassynews.ca/opinion/2015/06/09/canadian-values-are-ukrainian-values/47217.

43 On a state visit to Canada, Ukraine's president, Petro Poroshenko, expressed similar views. See: "'Canada is a friend indeed,' Ukrainian president tells Parliament," *CTV News*, 17 September 2014, https://www.ctvnews.ca/politics/canada-is-a-friend-indeed-ukrainian-president-tells-parliament-1.2010786.

126 Notes to pages 61–2

44 On diasporas and their potential for Canadian foreign policy, see: *Tapping Our Potential: Diaspora Communities and Canadian Foreign Policy* (Mosaic Institute/Walter and Duncan Gordon Foundation, 2011), http://mosaicinstitute.ca/wp-content/uploads/2016/05/7.pdf.

45 UCC, "Ukrainian Canadian Congress Launches Ukraine Appeal," 18 October 2015, PCUH Archives, Canada-Ukraine Project. For specific exmaples of community assistance projects, see: Tanya Talaga, "Ukrainian Canadians Answering the Call of the Homeland," *Toronto Star*, 22 December 2014; "Canadian Medical Team Returns to Ukraine," *Euromaidan Press*, 22 April 2015; Jason Warrick, "Saskatchewan Ambulances Arrive in Ukraine to Help War Wounded," *Saskatoon StarPhoenix*, 23 August 2015; and "Canadian Surgeons Operate on Ukrainian Soldiers Scarred by War," *Ukraine Today*, 27 October 2015. On provincial aid, see: "Ontario Pledges Help for Ukraine," *Ontario Newsroom*, 9 March 2014; Michael Franklin, "Alberta offering aid to Ukraine," CTV *Calgary*, 4 March 2014, https://calgary.ctvnews.ca/alberta-offering-aid-to-ukraine-1.1713039; and Government of Manitoba, "Manitoba Announces Humanitarian Assistance for Victims of Violence in Ukraine," news release, 23 February 2014, https://news.gov.mb.ca/news/print,index. html?archive=&item=20534.

46 Christian Borys, "Ukraine's other war: The fight to heal soldiers' bodies and minds," *Maclean's*, 22 June 2015, https://www.macleans.ca/news/world/ukraines-other-war-the-fight-to-heal-soldiers-bodies-and-minds/.

47 UCC, "Briefing Note to Members of Parliament: The Situation in Ukraine and Canada's Response," 9 February 2015, PCUH Archives, Canada-Ukraine Project.

48 Christian Borys, "Ukraine's other war." See also: Canada-Ukraine Foundation, "Canadian Doctors Rebuild Bodies Shattered by War," [n.d.], https://www.cufoundation.ca/humanitarian-medical/canadian-doctors-rebuild-bodies-shattered-by-war-in-ukraine/.

49 See: Ryan Maloney, "Ukraine Crisis: Most Canadians Satisfied with Harper's Response, Poll Suggests," *Huffington Post*, 6 May 2014, https://www.huffingtonpost.ca/2014/05/06/ukraine-crisis-canada-poll-harper-russia-putin_n_5269839.html; and Sonja Puzic, "Canadians back PM's Ukraine support, but split over fighting Islamic State: Poll,"

Notes to pages 65–7 127

CTV *News*, 4 September 2014, http://www.ctvnews.ca/politics/
canadians-back-pm-s-ukraine-support-but-split-over-fighting-islamic-
state-poll-1.1992242.

CHAPTER FOUR

1 Ripsman, Taliaferro, and Lobell, *Neoclassical Realist Theory
of International Politics*, 61–6.
2 Kenneth Whyte, "In Conversation: Stephen Harper," *Maclean's*, 5 July
2011, http://www.macleans.ca/general/how-he-sees-canadas-role-in-
the-world-and-where-he-wants-to-take-the-country-2/; John Ibbitson,
"With freedom eroding in Ukraine, PM puts his principles to work,"
Globe and Mail, 26 October 2010, http://www.theglobeandmail.com/
news/politics/with-freedom-eroding-in-ukraine-pm-puts-his-principles-
to-work/article4330293/; Keehn, "Stephen Harper, the Ottawa Attack,
and the Question of Canadian Security"; PMO, "Prime Minister
Harper's Remarks at a Reception in Honour of Czech Prime Minister
Mirek Topolánek," 29 February 2008, PCUH Archives, Canada-
Ukraine Project; and PMO, "Prime Minister Harper Congratulates
Former Prime Minister Brian Mulroney on Award at Ukrainian Tribute
Dinner," 18 April 2007, PCUH Archives, Canada-Ukraine Project.
3 Ken Boessenkool and Sean Speer, "Ordered Liberty: How Harper's
Philosophy Transformed Canada for the Better," *Policy Options*, 1
December 2015, http://policyoptions.irpp.org/2015/12/01/harper/.
4 See: Paul Wells, *The Longer I'm Prime Minister: Stephen Harper and
Canada, 2006–* (Toronto: Random House, 2013), 60; and Whyte,
"In Conversation: Stephen Harper."
5 The term "neoconservative," as applied to Harper, was typically meant
to be a pejorative, conforming to Max Boot's description of the term
as "an all-purpose term of abuse for anyone deemed to be hawkish."
See: Max Boot, "Neocons," *Foreign Policy*, February 2004, 20.
6 Boessenkool and Speer, "Ordered Liberty," 19. In a 2014 speech before
the United Nations General Assembly, Prime Minister Harper spoke
of Canada's willingness to "join with other civilized peoples and to
challenge affronts to international order, affronts to human dignity
itself, such as are today present in Eastern Europe." See: "Read
Stephen Harper's address to the UN General Assembly," *Toronto Star*,

128 Notes to pages 67–9

25 September 2014, https://www.thestar.com/news/canada/2014/09/25/read_stephen_harpers_address_to_the_un_general_assembly.html; and PMO, "PM Delivers Remarks at a Joint Press Conference with Chancellor Merkel," 27 March 2014, PCUH Archives, Canada-Ukraine Project.

7 Robert Kagan, *The Return of History and the End of Dreams* (New York: Vintage, 2009), 4.

8 Paul Wells, "Why Harper wants to take on the world."

9 Colin Robertson, "Harper's world view," *Policy Options*, October 2011, http://policyoptions.irpp.org/magazines/ the-new-normal-majority-government/harpers-world-view/.

10 "Read Stephen Harper's Address to the UN General Assembly."

11 This approach would have significant public appeal. See: Timothy B. Graville, Thomas J. Scotto, Jason Reifler, and Harold D. Clarke, "Foreign Policy Beliefs and Support for Stephen Harper and the Conservative Party," *Canadian Foreign Policy Journal* 20, no. 2 (2014): 11–30.

12 For a discussion of the Mulroney government's 1991 "Good Governance" initiative, see: Gecelovsky and Keating, "Liberal Internationalism for Conservatives," 197–205.

13 On international change and the socialization process, see: G. John Ikenberry and Charles A. Kupchan, "Socialization and Hegemonic Power," *International Organization* 44, no. 3 (1990): 283.

14 Ibid., 285.

15 See: PMO, "Prime Minister Harper's Remarks at a Reception in Honour of Mirek Topolánek."

16 Daryl Bricker and John Ibbitson use the term "Laurentian elites" to describe the Central Canadian political establishment that governed for most of the post–World War II period – a set of political and cultural elites that exercised hegemonic control over Canadian politics prior to the political ascent of the Harper Conservatives in 2006. See: Daryl Bricker and John Ibbitson, *The Big Shift: The Seismic Change in Canadian Politics, Business, and Culture and What It Means For Our Future* (Toronto: HarperCollins, 2014), 2–10. For a statement on the principles governing the Reform Party, see: Reform Party of Canada, *Platform & Statement of Principles*, 25.

Notes to pages 70–3

17 Christian Leuprecht suggests that Western Canadian conservatism has been influenced by the values that Americans brought with them when they immigrated to the Western provinces. Leuprecht associates Reform with Canadian neoconservatism, which he suggests "patterns itself after American conservatism." Christian Leuprecht, "The Tory Fragment in Canada: Endangered Species?," *Canadian Journal of Political Science* 36, no. 2 (2003): 409.

18 Tonda MacCharles, "Prime Minister Harper says Canada less protectionist than U.S., calls for Canadian Nationalism that's not Anti-American," *Toronto Star,* 19 November 2012, https://www.thestar.com/news/canada/2012/11/19/prime_minister_harper_says_canada_less_protectionist_than_us_calls_for_canadian_nationalism_thats_not_antiamerican.html.

19 John Ibbitson, *Stephen Harper* (New York: Signal, 2016), 335.

20 Wells, "Why Harper wants to take on the world."

21 Robertson, "Harper's world view."

22 For a statement on the pivotal role of the US in the post–Cold War world and the strain of leadership, see: Robert Kagan, "The Benevolent Empire," *Foreign Policy* 111 (summer 1998): 32–3.

23 Ibbitson, *Stephen Harper,* 335.

24 Ikenberry and Kupchan, "Socialization and Hegemonic Power," 284.

25 Bricker and Ibbitson, *The Big Shift,* 14.

26 Ibbitson, *Stephen Harper,* 330–1.

27 Prime Minister Harper characterized the Canada-US relationship as "perhaps the most important issue that ever faces Canada," describing the United States as Canada's "best ally" and "most consistent friend." He concluded: "we forget these things at our own peril." See: Paul Wells, "Living in a world without leaders," *Maclean's,* 18 June 2012, http://www.macleans.ca/uncategorized/living-in-a-world-without-leaders/.

28 Ibbitson, *Stephen Harper,* 325.

29 PMO, "Statement by the Prime Minister of Canada in Toronto, Tribute to Liberty Dinner."

30 PMO, "PM Delivers Remarks at Joint Press Conference with Prime Minister Yatsenyuk of Ukraine," 22 March 2014, PCUH Archives, Canada-Ukraine Project.

130 Notes to pages 73–6

31 Chapnick, "Peace, Order, and Good Government," 650.

32 Reform Party of Canada, *Platform & Statement of Principles*, 25.

33 Steven Chase, "Harper takes leading role in G7 against Russia," *Globe and Mail*, 28 March 2014, https://www.theglobeandmail. com/news/politics/harper-takes-leading-role-in-g7-against-russia/ article17727891/.

34 Chapnick, "Peace, Order, and Good Government," 648; and Massie and Roussel, "The Twilight of Internationalism?," 41.

35 Leslie MacKinnon, "John Baird Compares Russia's Actions in Ukraine to Nazi Invasion of Czechoslovakia," CBC *News*, 3 March 2014, http://www.cbc.ca/news/politics/john-baird-compares-russia-s-actions-in-ukraine-to-naziinvasion-of-czechoslovakia-1.2558118.

36 "Harper calls Putin 'extreme nationalist, imperialist,'" *Toronto Star*, 8 June 2014, https://www.thestar.com/news/canada/2014/06/08/ harper_calls_putin_extreme_nationalist_imperialist.html.

37 Paul Wells and John Geddes, "What you don't know about Stephen Harper," *Maclean's*, 31 January 2011, http://www.macleans.ca/news/ canada/what-you-dont-know-about-stephen-harper/.

38 Tom Parry, "Stephen Harper says he'll push for Russia's expulsion from the G8," CBC *News*, 22 March 2014, http://www.cbc.ca/news/ politics/stephen-harper-says-he-ll-push-for-russia-s-expulsion-from-the-g8-1.2583034.

39 PMO, "PM Delivers Remarks at Joint Press Conference with Prime Minister Yatsenyuk of Ukraine."

40 For a full discussion of this point, see: Kordan, *Strategic Friends*, 103–4.

41 Ibbitson, *Stephen Harper*, 333.

42 "The West Block," *Global News*, 8 June 2014, http://globalnews.ca/ news/1381283/transcript-episode-40-june-8/.

43 DFATD, "Address by Minister Baird to the NATO Council of Canada Conference – Ukraine: The Future of International Norms." See also: Michael Den Tandt, "Old foreign policy nostrums of Canada as 'honest broker' not just dead, but buried," *National Post*, 20 July 2014, http://nationalpost.com/opinion/michael-den-tandt-old-foreign-policy-nostrums-of-canada-as-honest-broker-not-just-dead-but-buried/wcm/ add89f1b-51f5-4c83-a499-7ed1c027230b.

44 For an excellent discussion of the philosophical origins of Stephen Harper's vision and argument against the ethical relativism of

Notes to pages 77–8

traditional liberals, see: Scott Staring, "Stephen Harper, Leo Strauss and the Politics of Fear," Centre for International Policy Studies, CIPS Working Paper, May 2015, https://www.cips-cepi.ca/publications/stephen-harper-leo-strauss-and-the-politics-of-fear-2/.

45 PMO, "Statement by the Prime Minister of Canada in Toronto, Tribute to Liberty Dinner."

46 DFATD, "Canada-Ukraine Relations," January 2015, PCUH Archives, Canada-Ukraine Project.

47 PMO, "Statement by the Prime Minister of Canada in Toronto, Tribute to Liberty Dinner."

48 Emma Fitzsimmons, "Putin Gets Cool Reception from G-20," *New York Times*, 15 November 2014; Ben Doherty, "G20: Canadian prime minister shirtfronts Vladimir Putin instead," *Guardian*, 15 November 2014, https://www.theguardian.com/world/2014/nov/15/g20-canadian-prime-minister-shirtfronts-vladimir-putin-instead; Jason Scott and Ilya Arkhipov, "Harper Uses Handshake to Tell Putin to 'Get Out of Ukraine,'" *Bloomberg*, 15 November 2014, https://www.bloomberg.com/news/articles/2014-11-15/harper-uses-handshake-to-tell-putin-he-must-get-out-of-ukraine-; Steven Chase, "Harper tells Putin to 'get out of Ukraine' in G20 encounter," *Globe and Mail*, 14 November 2014, www.theglobeandmail.com/news/politics/harper-and-g20-leaders-confront-putin-problem-at-australia-meet/article21603599/; and "Ukraine crisis: Russia under pressure at G20 summit," *BBC News*, 15 November 2014, http://www.bbc.co.uk/news/world-australia-30067612.

49 UCC, "Briefing Note to the Government of Canada." Public calls for lethal arms for Ukraine were numerous at the time, including by Derek Fraser, Canada's former ambassador to Ukraine. See: "Canada Urged to Support Ukraine with Lethal Weapons," *Ukrainain News*, 23 October–5 November 2014.

50 Prime Minister Harper, responding to criticism that the government was disingenuous in its support of a muscular foreign policy as evidenced by cuts to the defence budget, declared that Canada's contribution was measured in "capabilities" and not in "dollars." David Akin, "Harper on defence spending: 'Canada a major contributor,'" *Toronto Sun*, 27 May 2015, https://torontosun.com/2015/05/27/harper-on-defence-spending-canada-a-major-contributor/wcm/326dbe08-1c70-

132 Notes to pages 78–80

45db-b187-8ca58e4a12e8. For a critique of the Harper government's defence spending, see: J.L. Granatstein, "How the Harper government lost its way on defence spending," *Globe and Mail*, 1 October 2014.

51 Marie Danielle Smith, "Military aid to Ukraine was last-minute scramble under pressure from PM: Docs," *Hill Times*, 20 April 2016, https://www.hilltimes.com/2016/04/20/military-aid-to-ukraine-was-last-minute-scramble-under-pressure-from-pm-docs/58871.

52 Matthew Fisher, "Stephen Harper says Putin is stuck in Cold War as Obama warns of threat to world order," *National Post*, 26 March 2104, https://nationalpost.com/news/stephen-harper-says-putin-is-stuck-in-cold-war-as-obama-warns-of-threat-to-world-order.

53 Heinbecker, quoted in Jim Coyle, "John Baird a loyal lieutenant to Harper in time of uninspired foreign policy," *Toronto Star*, 6 February 2015, https://www.thestar.com/news/insight/2015/02/06/john-baird-a-loyal-lieutenant-to-harper-in-time-of-uninspired-foreign-policy.html.

54 Stephen Harper, "PM Delivers Remarks at the United for Ukraine Gala."

55 Ibid. See also: PMO, "PM Delivers Remarks at a Joint Press Conference with Chancellor Merkel"; PMO, "Statement by the Prime Minister in Toronto, Tribute to Liberty Dinner"; PMO, "PM Welcomes Ukrainian President Petro Poroshenko to Canada," 17 September 2014, PCUH Archives, Canada-Ukraine Project; and Stephen Harper, "Our duty is to stand firm in the face of Russian aggression," *Globe and Mail*, 25 July 2014, https://www.theglobeandmail.com/opinion/our-duty-is-to-stand-firm-in-the-face-of-russian-aggression/article19767742/.

56 See: John Ibbitson, "Trudeau's foreign policy vs. Harper's: There is little difference," *Globe and Mail*, 8 March 2017, https://www.theglobeandmail.com/news/politics/trudeau-taking-foreign-policy-cue-from-tory-playbook/article34241539/; and Roger Annis, "Canada's Political Mainstream Backs War in Ukraine," *Counterpunch*, 31 March 2015, https://www.counterpunch.org/2015/03/31/canadas-political-mainstream-backs-war-in-ukraine/. See also: Matthew Fisher, "Thomas Mulcair gives few clues to Canada's foreign policy under an NDP government," *National Post*, 15 June 2015, PCUH Archives, Canada-Ukraine Project; Kathryn Blaze Carlson, "Ukrainian Canadians have a strong voice in Ottawa," *Globe and Mail*, 1 February 2014, https://www.theglobeandmail.com/news/politics/ukrainian-canadians-have-

Notes to pages 81–8

a-strong-voice-in-ottawa/article16647646/; and "Tale of the Tape: Read a Full Transcript of Maclean's Debate [on foreign policy]," *Maclean's*, 7 August 2015, https://www.macleans.ca/politics/ottawa/tale-of-the-tape-read-a-full-transcript-of-macleans-debate/.

57 Chrystia Freeland, "Why Canada should support Ukraine's democratic protestors," *Globe and Mail*, 26 January 2014, https://www.theglobeandmail.com/opinion/why-canada-should-support-ukraines-democratic-protesters/article16507240/.

CHAPTER FIVE

1 Power transition theory posits that a preponderant coalition of status quo powers is the best guarantor of peace. See: Ronald L. Tammen, "The Organski Legacy: A Fifty-Year Research Program," *International Interactions* 34, no. 4 (2008): 315–18. Roy Rempel, a former advisor to the Harper government, maintains that Canada can maximize its influence by working closely with the United States. Rempel, *Dreamland*, 2.

2 Canada's deployment of 200 military trainers to Ukraine positioned it at the forefront of the coalition's response to the crisis. Here, Canada's contributions exceeded those of the UK and rivalled those of the US. See: "Ukraine crisis: Canada sending 200 trainers for Ukraine military," *CBC News*, 14 April 2015, http://www.cbc.ca/news/politics/ukraine-crisis-canada-sending-200-trainers-for-ukraine-military-1.3031806.

3 For public poll results, see: Puzic, "Canadians back PM's Ukraine support, but split over fighting Islamic State: poll."

4 "'Canada forged in the fires of First World War': Stephen Harper marks anniversary of historic conflict," *National Post*, 4 August 2014, https://nationalpost.com/news/canada/canada-forged-in-the-fires-of-first-world-war-stephen-harper-marks-anniversary-of-historic-conflict.

5 See the transcript of Prime Minister Harper's speech in the House of Commons during President Petro Poroshenko's visit: "Harper: Canada stands behind Ukraine," *Calgary Herald*, 18 September 2014, https://calgaryherald.com/opinion/harper-canada-stands-behind-ukraine.

6 Andrew Coyne, "The Harper Leadership Cult," *Maclean's*, 22 September 2008, https://archive.macleans.ca/article/2008/9/22/the-harper-leaders-iip-cult.

134 Notes to pages 88–90

7 See: Duane Bratt, "Implementing the Reform Party Agenda: The Roots of Stephen Harper's Foreign Policy," *Canadian Foreign Policy Journal* 24, no. 1(2018): 1–17.

8 For a discussion of this transition, see: Leuprecht, "The Tory Fragment in Canada," 407–11.

9 For an analysis of Stephen Harper's objections to international institutions and multilateralism, see: Staring, "Stephen Harper, Leo Strauss and the Politics of Fear." See also: John Ibbitson, *The Big Break: The Conservative Transformation of Canada's Foreign Policy*, Centre for International Governance Innovation, CIGI Papers 29, 7 April 2014, https://www.cigionline.org/sites/default/files/cigi_paper_29.pdf.

10 Several personalities associated with Canada's orthodox foreign policy establishment were hyper-critical of the Harper government's pro-Euromaidan Ukraine policy, understating the threat while ignoring system requirements. See: David Pugliese, "Harper Government Response on Ukraine Just Bluster, Say Former Ambassadors – Canada Increasingly Marginalized on World Stage," *Ottawa Citizen*, 2 March 2014; and John Ibbitson, "Harper's foreign policy: Ukraine and the Diaspora vote," Centre for International Governance Innovation, 19 March 2014, https://www.cigionline.org/articles/harpers-foreign-policy-ukraine-and-diaspora-vote.

11 The goal of Canadian foreign policy, Stephen Harper declared, was "no longer just to go along and get along with everyone else's agenda. It is no longer to please every dictator with a vote at the United Nations." Foreign Minister John Baird echoed Harper in a speech to the UN, articulating the sentiment that Canada would no longer abide by a "go along to get along" approach. For the text of Baird's speech, see: Aaron Wherry, "Canada does not just 'go along' in order to 'get along,'" *Maclean's*, 26 September 2011, https://www.macleans.ca/politics/ottawa/canada-does-not-just-go-along-in-order-to-get-along/. Harper rationalized this approach by suggesting that Canada's foreign policy tradition had often consisted of acquiescence to the international community's "bad ideas." Stephen Harper, *Right Here, Right Now: Politics and Leadership in the Age of Disruption* (Toronto: Signal/McClelland & Stewart, 2018), 127.

12 Harper, *Right Here, Right Now*, 127; and Paul Wells, "Why Harper wants to take on the world."

Notes to pages 91–3

13 See, for example: Paul Grod, "Ukraine needs NATO's weapons, not its words," *Globe and Mail*, 3 September 2014, https://www.theglobeandmail.com/opinion/ukraine-needs-natos-weapons-not-its-words/article20321269/#dashboard/follows/; L. Luciuk, "Canada Should Send Troops to Ukraine," *Winnipeg Free Press*, 9 Septmeber 2014, https://www.winnipegfreepress.com/opinion/analysis/canada-should-send-troops-to-ukraine-274435131.html; and Oksana Bashuk Hepburn, "Ukraine therefore needs overt help," *Hill Times*, 6 October 2014, https://www.hilltimes.com/2014/10/06/ukraine-therefore-needs-overt-military-help/29806/39806.

14 As quoted in Stephen Chase, "Harper Commemorates 100th Anniversary of the First World War," *Globe and Mail*, 4 August 2014, https://www.theglobeandmail.com/news/national/harper-marks-100th-anniversary-of-wwi-critical-conflict-in-canadian-history/article19906944/.

15 See: Stephen Chase, "MH17: Ottawa blames Putin for downed Malaysian airliner," *Globe and Mail*, 21 July 2014, https://www.theglobeandmail.com/news/politics/mh17-ottawa-blames-putin-for-downed-malaysian-airliner/article19689234/; and Gloria Galloway, "MH17: Foreign Affairs Minister Baird discusses airline tragedy, seeking justice," *Globe and Mail*, 21 July 2014, https://www.theglobeandmail.com/news/politics/mh17-foreign-affairs-minister-john-baird-discusses-airline-tragedy-next-steps/article19687780/.

16 See: PMO, "Statement by the Prime Minister of Canada in Toronto, Tribute to Liberty Dinner." See also: Paul Wells, "Harper, Communism and the lessons of memory," *Maclean's*, 2 June 2014, https://www.macleans.ca/politics/ottawa/harper-communism-and-the-lessons-of-memory/.

17 Stephen Harper, "Our duty is to stand firm in the face of Russian aggression."

18 This form of thinking is comparable to a strain of liberalism that emerged during the Cold War, which Judith Shklar describes as a "Liberalism of fear." See: Judith Shklar, "The Liberalism of Fear," in *Liberalism and the Moral Life*, ed. Nancy L. Rosenblum (Cambridge, MA: Harvard University Press, 1989), 21–37.

19 See: Staring, "Stephen Harper, Leo Strauss and the Politics of Fear."

20 The call "To freedom, ours and yours!" was heard on the barricades of the Euromaidan. See the text of the speech delivered by Josef Zissels,

136   Note to page 95

leader of the Congress of Ethnic Communities of Ukraine and head
of the Association of Jewish Communities of Ukraine, to the People's
Assembly of the Euromaidan on the Day of Dignity, 15 December
2013, https://www.ukma.edu.ua/eng/index.php/news/482-speech-
of-josef-zissels-at-euromaidan.

21 Comment by Rob Nicholson, Minister of Defence, at the 2014
International Security Forum in Halifax. "Defence Minister echoes
Harper's call for Russia to get out of Ukraine," *Maclean's,*
22 November 2014, https://www.macleans.ca/news/world/
defence-minister-says-russia-should-get-out-of-ukraine/.

Index

Afghanistan, 28, 70
agency, 5, 10, 64, 66, 82, 88
aid and assistance: ceasefire support and monitoring, 59, 78, 103, 105; as foreign policy instrument, 49; to Ukraine, 56, 61, 88, 100. *See also* Antonyshyn, Oleh; Operation Reassurance; Operation Unifier; sanctions
Alexander, Chris, 107
Andreychuk, Raynell. *See* election monitoring
Antonyshyn, Oleh, 62
appeasement, 74, 90
Axworthy, Lloyd, 115n30

Baird, John, 76, 97–8, 103–5, 112n4, 134n11; and global liberal order, 37–8; and rhetoric, 55; and Russia, 38
Bennett, Andrew, 97, 103
Bezan, James, 100, 103
Brisbane Summit, 77

Brown, Lois, 101
Budapest Memorandum, 23, 32, 36, 40, 75, 115n27
Bush, George W., 34

Canada: and global liberal order, x, 9, 13–15, 18–19, 21, 37, 42–3, 48, 57, 63, 68, 71, 74, 78, 84, 87, 94–5; as middle power, 14, 16, 24, 42, 113n9; political culture, values, and identity, 3–4, 10–11, 14–15, 46, 48, 50, 52, 54–5, 68, 77, 79–81, 83, 87; and Russia, ix, x, 3, 5–6, 11, 35, 37–8, 46, 51, 54, 57, 74, 77, 98, 107; and Ukraine, xiii, 3, 8–9, 14, 22–7, 38–9, 40, 43, 52–3, 56, 77, 80, 85, 87, 95, 107, 109, 111n2, 115n29, 125n43; and United States, 17–19, 22–3, 33, 35, 39, 41, 50, 66, 69, 71–2, 75, 84–5, 121n9, 121n14, 129n27, 133n1. *See also* aid and assistance; coalition; foreign policy (Canada); sanctions

Canada-Ukraine Chamber of Commerce, 41

Canada-Ukraine Free Trade Agreement (CUFTA), 55, 100, 109, 124n31

Carment, David, 60

Chapnick, Adam, 73

Chrétien, Jean, 71

classical liberalism, 48, 50, 66–7

coalition, 31–4, 40–1, 63, 117n12, 133n1; Canada as part of, 10, 13, 15, 17–21, 27, 36, 42–3, 46–8, 50, 57–9, 64, 76–8, 84–5, 87, 90–2, 94, 133n2; and sanctions, 35, 56, 78, 84; and status quo, 7, 9, 11, 13–16, 19, 20–1, 28, 31, 33, 70, 72, 74, 84–5, 94, 116n4, 120n5, 133n1; Ukraine and, 14, 22–4, 27, 31, 38–9. *See also* Russia; United States

Cold War, ix, 6, 9, 12–15, 18–19, 20, 26, 29, 48, 51, 69, 76, 85, 135n18

Conservative Party of Canada, 69–73, 81–2, 86, 121n14. *See also* Harper, Stephen; Reform Party of Canada

Crimea: referendum, 98; and Russian aggression, 6, 31–2, 38, 84, 118n19; and sanctions, 99–100, 108

denuclearization. *See* Ukraine

deterrence, 16, 31, 33, 35, 39–40, 56, 58, 99, 102

Donbas. *See* insurgency

election monitoring, 60, 87, 99–100, 103, 106

elite socialization, 69–72, 81, 89

Euromaidan, 5, 53, 55, 70–1, 81, 93, 97, 99, 118n19, 134n10, 135n20

European Union, 35, 118n26

Fast, Ed, 100, 105

foreign policy (Canada), ix–xi, 4, 6, 8–10, 12, 29, 85–6, 88, 111n2, 121n14, 134n10; Brian Mulroney and, 21–3; Canada-Ukraine Free Trade Agreement, 55, 100, 109, 124n31; national interest and, ix, 4, 9, 44–5, 48, 57, 60, 83, 88, 90; Pearsonian tradition and, 48–9, 71–2, 89–90; and public opinion, 34–5, 43, 63; and sanctions, 57; Stephen Harper and, 46–52, 54, 75, 77–9, 81, 88–90, 94, 123n29, 131n50, 134n11; symbolism and, 52–3, 78, 87; and United States, 16, 18, 70–3; and values, 10, 14–15, 46, 49, 51, 55, 60, 61–9, 87–8, 94, 120n7. *See also* Heinbecker, Paul; Laurentian consensus and elites; Trudeau, Pierre Elliott

Fraser, Derek, 131n49

Freeland, Chrystia, 3, 80–1, 111n2

Freezing Assets of Corrupt Foreign Officials Act. *See* sanctions

G7/G8, 15, 53–4, 85, 98, 101, 103, 107, 116n3, 120n2

G20 Brisbane Summit, 77

Germany, 34, 124n37; and invasion of Czechoslovakia, 74, 76

global liberal order, 9, 13–14, 16–17, 20, 47–8, 51–2, 67, 72, 75, 90, 94, 112n3; consolidation of, 9, 21, 84; expansion of, 13, 24, 26–7; in post–Cold War era, 27, 29, 39, 88. *See also* Canada; coalition; Harper, Stephen; international system; liberal democracy

Globe and Mail, 101

Gorbachev, Mikhail, 20

Gray, Charlotte, 51

Grod, Paul, 61, 97, 107

Harper, Stephen: and Canadian identity, 11, 48–9, 50, 52, 69, 80, 83, 87, 94; and commemorative ceremonies, 68; and Euromaidan, 53, 70–1, 99; and global liberal order, 10, 46, 51, 75, 92–3; and ideology, 10–11, 49, 60, 66–7, 69, 73, 79, 82, 92; and Laurentian consensus, 71, 82, 89–90; leadership of, 4–6, 10, 66, 77, 94; and "moral clarity," 6, 76, 112; and political culture, 10, 55, 63, 80, 91; political realism of, 49, 67–8; and Reform Party, 49, 73, 88; rhetoric, 6, 8–9, 41–2, 47, 66, 78, 85; and Russia, ix, 3, 6, 9, 36, 49, 109; on sanctions, 38, 57, 100–1, 105; on

sovereignty and independence, 8–9, 42, 53, 57, 59, 74, 78–9, 91, 98, 101, 104, 109; and United States, 50, 70–1, 90, 121n9, 129n27; values, 5, 10, 46, 49, 62, 67–8, 69, 73, 78–80, 82–3, 87, 93; views on history, 6, 52, 60; visits to Ukraine, 53, 93, 99, 107; and Vladimir Putin, 34, 75–6, 79. *See also* foreign policy (Canada); G20 Brisbane Summit; *Globe and Mail*; Ukrainian-Canadian community

Harris, Mike. *See* election monitoring

Heinbecker, Paul, 79

Hollande, François, 31

House of Commons of Canada, 103, 106

illiberalism, 29, 47–8, 92

institutional signalling, 25, 114n26

insurgency, 6, 91–2, 101, 103, 105; and Russia, 36, 40, 91, 98

International Monetary Fund, 99

International Peacekeeping and Security Centre (Yavoriv, Ukraine), 102, 108–9

international system, ix, xi, 12–13, 16, 26, 29–30, 37, 51, 60, 67; structure of, 5, 7, 10, 15, 28

international terrorism, 51

Iraq, 28, 32, 34, 70, 71

Index

Johnston, David, 54
Juncker, Jean-Claude, 104

Kenney, Jason, 39, 54, 106–8
Klimkin, Pavlo, 107

Landry, Joseph, 60
Laurentian consensus and elites,
    69–73, 128n16. *See also*
    Harper, Stephen; Reform Party
    of Canada; United States
Lavrov, Sergei, 60
liberal democracy: and global
    liberal order, 15–16, 26, 50;
    and political leadership, 15
Liberal Party of Canada, 49, 81,
    89. *See also* parliamentary
    opposition (Canada); Trudeau,
    Justin
Libya, 30, 75, 123n29

Malaysia Airlines flight MH17,
    36, 91–2, 101, 109
Merkel, Angela, 105
Minsk Agreements, 59, 78, 103,
    105, 124n37
Mulcair, Thomas, 80
Mulroney, Brian: and Cold War,
    15; end of Cold War, 21–2, 68,
    114n19; and Ukraine, 22, 25;
    and Ukrainian-Canadian com-
    munity, 25; and United States,
    68, 71. *See also* foreign policy
    (Canada)

NATO, 85, 102, 104. *See also*
    Operation Reassurance

neoclassical realism, 7–8, 28, 42,
    45, 47, 64, 81, 85–6; and deci-
    sion makers, 64, 81; and
    domestic politics, 45, 47; and
    the international system, 28, 42
New Democratic Party, 80–1. *See
    also* Mulcair, Thomas; parlia-
    mentary opposition (Canada)
Nicholson, Rob, 95, 102, 104–6

Obama, Barack, 39, 41, 70, 98;
    rhetoric, 117n12, 118n23,
    118n25
Onyschuk, Bob, 41
Operation Reassurance (NATO),
    58–9, 99, 102, 104, 106–8
Operation Unifier (Canadian
    Armed Forces), 59, 87, 91, 109
Organization for Security and
    Cooperation in Europe
    (OSCE), 59, 85, 87, 97–100,
    104, 106, 120n2

Paradis, Christian, 100
parliamentary opposition
    (Canada), 80, 86
Parubiy, Andriy, 105
political culture, 4, 7, 14–15,
    45–6, 50, 94. *See also* Canada;
    Harper, Stephen
political realism, ix. *See also*
    Harper, Stephen
Poroshenko, Petro, 53, 100, 103,
    107
Progressive Conservative Party of
    Canada, 49, 89. *See also*
    Mulroney, Brian

Index

Putin, Vladimir, 30–1; criticism of, 38, 41; and Ukraine, 53–4, 118n19, 118n26. *See also* G20 Brisbane Summit; Harper, Stephen

Reform Party of Canada: critique of Laurentian consensus, 69–70, 89; on foreign policy, 49, 69, 73, 120n7; principles, 48–9, 88–9, 92; and United States, 69, 70, 129n17

Russia: aggression against Ukraine, 5–6, 58, 62, 67, 98, 104; deterrence against, 39–41, 43, 56, 78, 94, 102; and global liberal order and security, 8–10, 28, 36–7, 42, 46, 48, 50–1, 57, 60–1, 65, 75, 84, 88, 91, 116n3, 116n9, 117n12, 118n25; and revisionism, 29–30, 32–3, 38, 49, 72, 74, 92, 116n4; sanctions against, 32–3, 35, 38, 40, 56, 90. *See also* Canada; Crimea; Harper, Stephen; insurgency; Putin, Vladimir; sanctions; United States

sanctions: Freezing Assets of Corrupt Foreign Officials Act, 99; Special Economic Measures Act, 56, 108; special measures, 56–7, 80, 87, 99–101, 103, 105. *See also* coalition; Harper, Stephen; Russia

Savchenko, Nadiya, 106, 108

Soviet Union, 9, 12–13, 19–20, 29–30, 48; collapse of, 20–3, 26, 67–9. *See also* Gorbachev, Mikhail

Special Economic Measures Act. *See* sanctions

Stairs, Denis, 14

status quo. *See* coalition

Sudetenland. *See* Germany

Syria, 30–1

Thatcher, Margaret, 6, 67, 72, 75

Tories. *See* Progressive Conservative Party of Canada

Toronto Star, 37, 104

transatlantic alliance, 15

Trudeau, Justin, 3, 80

Trudeau, Pierre Elliott, 19

Turchynov, Oleksandr, 99

Ukraine: crisis, x, 5, 31, 37, 62, 87, 92–3, 98, 105; and denuclearization, 14, 23, 25–7, 40, 75, 114n25, 115n29; and post–Cold War order, 27, 38–9, 77, 82, 84, 91, 95; reforms in, 22, 25, 39–40, 43, 56, 103, 105, 108; sovereignty and independence, 9, 23, 32, 36, 38, 42, 53, 57, 59, 88, 104; in transition, 24–7, 88, 119n30. *See also* aid and assistance; Budapest Memorandum; Canada; coalition; foreign policy (Canada); Russia; United States

Index

Ukrainian-Canadian community, x, xiii, 24, 27, 111n2; assistance to Ukraine, 61–2; electoral influence, 86; and Harper government, x, 8, 10, 43, 46, 61, 78, 86, 88, 91, 98, 102; and Russia, 88. *See also* Ukrainian Canadian Congress

Ukrainian Canadian Congress, 40, 61–2, 102. *See also* Grod, Paul

United Nations, 15, 120n2, 134n11; Stephen Harper at, 127n6

United States, 17–19, 21–2, 34, 50, 67, 69–70, 115n27; and Laurentian elites, 71–3, 77; as leader of international system, 16–19, 28, 30, 40, 58, 67–9, 72, 75, 82, 85, 87; military assistance to Ukraine, 39, 58–9, 75–6; retrenchment, 28, 30–1, 33, 35, 41–2, 66, 70, 76, 90; and Russia, 33, 37, 39, 116n4, 117n12; and Soviet Union, 12–13, 21; Stephen Harper and, 10, 50, 70–1, 73–5, 77, 82, 121n9, 129n27. *See also* Bush, George W.; Canada; foreign policy (Canada); Obama, Barack

values. *See* Canada; Harper, Stephen

Van Rompuy, Herman, 104

Yanukovych, Viktor, 5, 52, 97, 99, 108

Yatsenyuk, Arseniy, 99

Yeltsin, Boris, 30

Yushchenko, Viktor, 52